Abbey,
I LOVE YOU!

FRESH
LEADERSHIP

I hope you enjoy!

XXOO —

Sarah

FRESH LEADERSHIP

5 SKILLS TO TRANSFORM YOU AND YOUR TEAM

Lead with Powerful New Insights and Tools for Today

SARAH K. ROBINSON

Niche Pressworks
Indianapolis

Fresh Leadership: Five Skills to Transform You and Your Team
ISBN 978-1-946533-45-6 (paperback)
ISBN 978-1-946533-46-3 (ebook)

Copyright © 2019 by Sarah K. Robinson

All rights reserved. No part of this book may be used or reproduced in any manner whatsoever without prior written consent of the author, except as provided by the United States of America copyright law.

Sarah K. Robinson does not claim to be employed by, affiliated with, or sponsored by Gallup. All non-Gallup information has not been approved and is not sanctioned or endorsed by Gallup in any way. Opinions, views, and interpretations of Gallup research are solely the beliefs of Sarah K. Robinson.

For permission to reprint portions of this content or bulk purchases, contact Sarah K. Robinson at sarah@freshconceptsonline.com.

Published by Niche Pressworks, Indianapolis, IN
http://NichePressworks.com

Printed in the United States of America

DEDICATION

To three leaders I love dearly: Dawson, Jack and Hope.

To my patient and insightful first reader, David.

CONTENTS

Dedication v
Preface xiii
Introduction 1

Section One

Mind the Gap 17
    Addressing the Gap 21
    Unwritten Rules and Unwritten Needs 21
    Old Work Rules and New Work Needs 22
    Summary 26
    Turning New Knowledge into Results 26

Today's Expectations 29
    Expectations Have Changed 29
    Friendship Expectations 33
    Teamwork Expectations 35
    Meaningful Work Expectations 40
    Summary 40
    Turning New Knowledge into Results 41

Section Two: F.R.E.S.H.

F.R.E.S.H. Feedback 45
- How Do You Handle Feedback? 45
- U.S. Schools Hardwire Our Need for Feedback 46
- Effective Feedback 49
- The Dreaded Annual Review 55
- Frequent Feedback Strategy 57
- Criticism or Critique? 60
- Summary 61
- Turning New Knowledge into Results 62

F.R.E.S.H. Rewards 65
- Everyone Wants the Right Birthday Cake 65
- Leaders Are Pseudo-Parents at Work 66
- Types of Rewards 67
- Traditional Rewards Theory 68
- Motivation Theory 69
- Type X and Type I 71
- Summary 73
- Turning New Knowledge into Results 73

F.R.E.S.H. Engagement 75
- Employee Engagement Versus Employee Satisfaction 75
- What Does Engagement Look Like? 76

- To Measure or to Not Measure 81
- Not a Silver Bullet 82
- Follow-Up Plans 83
- Choose Leaders Wisely 85
- Summary 89
- Turning New Knowledge into Results 89

F.R.E.S.H. Service 91
- The Servant-Leader Paradox 91
- Service—Why Now? 93
- Finding Your Why and Their Why 100
- Summary 102
- Turning New Knowledge into Results 102

F.R.E.S.H. Human Connection 105
- The Difference Between Being Frail and Being Vulnerable ... 105
- Vulcans at Work No More 108
- Emotional Intelligence is a Leadership Imperative 109
- Loneliness at Work Is an Epidemic 112
- The Dopamine-Social Media Mix-up 114
- Summary 116
- Turning New Knowledge into Results 117

Section Three

Who's Got Your Blind Spots? 121
- Being a Leader in Life 122
- All Drivers Have Blind Spots 123
- Who Challenges You Most? 126
- Empower the Team's Introvert 129
- Beware: The Curse of Knowledge 130
- Summary 132
- Turning New Knowledge into Results 133

Grow or Die 135
- Limiting Beliefs Can Limit Learning 136
- Model the Right Learning Behaviors 139
- Summary 142
- Turning New Knowledge into Results 142

Final Thoughts 145

BET and BEAR 147

Motivators at Work 149

Autonomy-Mastery-Purpose 150

Work and Meaning Inventory 152

Values 154

Loneliness Quiz 156

Thank You 160
About the Author 161

PREFACE

The Why Behind This Book

F.R.E.S.H. is an acronym that—like most good ideas I've ever had—popped into my head and refused to leave. It was 2010, and I had been working in the field of organizational behavior for about twenty years and teaching organizational behavior concepts to college students since 2002. My students frequently told me or wrote within their papers that they "wished their manager could take this class."

I'm not completely naïve. Initially, I suspected that this comment was just a few desperate students attempting to flatter their instructor and potentially improve their grade. However, after hearing this comment more than a handful of times, I decided it needed further consideration.

I wondered, **"What could I teach—when freed from the academic requirements that I was normally bound to—that would catapult mediocre managers into a new stratosphere of highly effective leadership?"** Once I asked myself this question, **the answer seemed obvious: it was a combination of topics that would help managers to become both book smart and street smart when it came to leadership.**

What I mean by this is that I frequently interact with leaders (many of whom have no advanced degrees or special training) who are extremely savvy when it comes to understanding how to motivate and inspire their team members. These leaders have leadership **street** smarts as opposed to leadership **book** smarts. However, I have also worked with leaders who have multiple advanced degrees in business or organizational behavior who have used their impressive book smarts to create a successful team. Of course, it is the rare and exceptional leader who has both—leadership street smarts and leadership book smarts.

Leadership street smarts is not normally taught in classrooms. Despite the lack of formal training, I have found that the qualities of a street-smart leader become obvious when I interact and coach leaders or prospective leaders who possess these qualities. And, they are even more obvious to those who are led by such leaders. For example, the street-smart leader often will intuitively understand the emotions of others, may see hidden gifts and talents of her employees, or may recognize how to cultivate relationships to bring out the full potential of the team.

As a college instructor, I was keenly aware that our class discussions kept circling back around to the same issues, regardless of what our syllabus indicated our day's focus should be. Despite my efforts to keep the group interested in individual differences, personality, perception, ethics, creativity, decision-making, motivation, communication, group dynamics, conflict, stress, or politics, we seemed to stray back to a few "hot" topics.

In 2011, when I renamed my consulting business FRESH Concepts, Inc., my plan was to share my combined consulting know-how (i.e., real-life experience) and my academic knowledge (Industrial and Organizational Psychology background) with the world.

Although it seemed obvious to me that there is an overlap between what is taught in academia and what is done in real life, it seemed that this connection was missing for aspiring leaders. I asked myself: How could current or aspiring leaders connect the academic and real-life dots? They were challenged with not only doing their current job but also synthesizing the learned and observed workplace behaviors that might help them drive their team to a higher level.

The acronym FRESH was inspired by my hope that these academic and real-life insights could be combined in a meaningful way. On the next page is a brief overview of the FRESH Leadership perspective.

F.R.E.S.H. Leadership	Leaders with *Book Smarts* understand that:	Leaders with *Street Smarts* understand that:
F – **Feedback**	Employees need information about how well they are doing to achieve goals. Good and poor performance is discussed.	Employees cannot improve without feedback. Street-smart leaders recognize the importance of specific, timely, positive, and performance-based feedback.
R – **Rewards**	Rewards and motivation are connected. Understanding the individual intrinsic and extrinsic motivators for each team member is the job of the leader.	External rewards (like money) are just one piece of motivating employees. Knowing what each employee values is key to harnessing motivation. Rewards should be aligned with individual values.
E – **Engagement**	Only 33% of American workers are engaged. Engaged workers have higher productivity, profitability, customer loyalty, and overall life satisfaction.	Having engaged employees is a leader's first priority. By identifying employees' skills and thoughtfully placing and developing employees, street-smart leaders increase a team's engagement. They know how to put the right people in the right seat on the bus.

F.R.E.S.H. Leadership	Leaders with Book Smarts understand that:	Leaders with Street Smarts understand that:
S – Service	Servant leadership is based on the premise that leaders should serve first and consciously lead later.	Serving employees is possible by giving meaning to their work. Addressing the organization's "why" and each employee's "why" are a leader's job.
H – Human Connection	Emotional intelligence (EI) allows leaders to connect with employees on a human level. Leaders with high levels of EI understand their own emotions, the emotions of others, and regulate emotions to enhance living.	Workplace loneliness is on the rise. Street-smart leaders know this is not a personal issue, it is an organizational issue that can have a far-reaching impact on the morale and productivity of the team.

In the chapters ahead, we'll look at each of these principles and practices individually, detailing why they are important to effective leadership.

INTRODUCTION

If your actions inspire others to dream more, learn more, do more and become more, you are a leader.

– John Quincy Adams

A middle-aged businessman learned, only ten days before he was to take his new position as CEO, that his business was on the verge of bankruptcy. At the outset, his executive team considered him an unsophisticated and second-rate leader. His employees had mixed feelings about his abilities. Even his board of directors questioned his aptitude, despite the years of hard work and dedication he had shown in his field.

Remarkably, after only four years in his position, he had pulled his company back from the brink of disaster. Despite three tumultuous years of waging a war against bankruptcy and numerous issues with his executive team, his business had turned the corner and come out stronger than ever in the fourth year.

The CEO finally found—after multiple tries—a fantastic right-hand man in the form of a vice president of operations. After many false starts, he had found the "general" who would follow through on plans and recommendations given to him.

The success of the company quickly and positively impacted the feelings and attitudes of everyone who knew the CEO, but especially those of the executives, the employees, and the board of directors. Soon, he was one of the most revered leaders among his peers. His leadership characteristics and traits became a model for all around him. Unfortunately, soon after this remarkable success, the CEO was murdered.

Who was this great leader, this amazingly successful CEO with an untimely death? The protagonist of this story is not the CEO of a company, but a past President of the United States, whose work and leadership traits I rely upon frequently as a corporate coach and college instructor.

He was not waging a war against corporate bankruptcy—he was engaged in a civil war. He was not lacking support from an executive team, employees, and board of directors. He was in desperate need of support from his cabinet members, soldiers, and the American people.

Abraham Lincoln needed more than a capable vice president of operations—he needed to find a relentless general for his Army. Once General Ulysses S. Grant, Lincoln's thirteenth general, was able to end the Civil War, President Abraham Lincoln was embraced by those who had questioned his abilities most. As a result of his decisions, he has become the most written-about non-religious leader in history.

After only one term as President, Lincoln had clear and irrefutably positive results. However, I question whether Lincoln would have been lauded as the remarkable leader that he was if the Civil War had not ended during his term and if he had not managed to reconcile our nation. It is only because of Lincoln's unfathomable success that his naysayers and antagonists were forced to relinquish their questioning stance and diminishing remarks.

And, it is only with twenty-twenty hindsight that historians have analyzed and elaborated upon Lincoln's leadership traits, that include authenticity, persuasion, integrity, storytelling, and visionary thought (to name only a few that have been written about at length).

To be a great leader, one must accomplish great things, have personality characteristics that are inspiring, and create a strong team. One will not be remembered as a great leader unless the goals of the group have been achieved. Similarly, one will not be memorable to the people he or she has led unless those people consider their leader to be an admirable person who has helped them accomplish great things.

If time travel were possible, could Abraham Lincoln capably replace Sheryl Sandberg as COO of Facebook? Would Julius Caesar, Napoleon Bonaparte, or Winston Churchill rise to the top of the 21st century leadership heap if they relied upon the same leadership attributes and qualities that they used during their lifetimes to lead today?

Leadership is certainly different now than when these historical leaders held the reins. And, importantly, it has even changed significantly since the late 1980s and 1990s, when many current leaders were coming up in the ranks.

Some of these changes are the result of practical, technical, or financial shifts that have occurred in the corporate world. For example, today there are many more jobs offering services (89%) versus those related to products. There is TWICE the need for skilled workers who perform jobs that require flexibility, creativity, and problem-solving than in the '80s and '90s.[1] And, pensions are no longer considered a normal benefit for full-time employees.

---

[1] O'Donnell, J.T. "A New Study Says Older Generations and Millennials Want the Same Thing in a Job--But That's Not Entirely True." *Inc.com*, Inc., 16 Apr. 2018, www.inc.com/jt-odonnell/a-new-study-says-older-generations-millennials-want-same-thing-in-a-job-but-thats-not-entirely-true.html.

There have also been demographic changes that have greatly impacted the workforce during this same period. For example, people are working and living longer than ever before; the US has more immigrants in the workforce than ever before; the family household size is shrinking (today the average family size is 2.5 people, as compared to 3+ people 50 years ago, and 4+ people a century ago); and fewer people under 30 years old are getting married.[2]

These market and demographic changes have impacted how leaders create successful teams. What's interesting is that, although the rules for creating a great team have shifted to accommodate these changes, there is no new rule book to share with today's experienced CEOs or tomorrow's leaders.

Can you imagine this happening in the sports world? Say, for example, the NBA decided to change the distance of the three-point line that currently ranges from 22 feet (corners) to 23.75 feet (top of the key). How might this change impact the game? How would things change for the players, coaches, referees, and rulebooks? My guess is that the players would start practicing differently; the coaches would set up new plays; the refs would familiarize themselves with the new rules; and the rulebooks would become quickly updated with the new ranges. Right?

While the demands of the workforce are different today than they were 25 years ago, the employers' rules, tools, and behaviors have not changed. The millennial generation has been the scapegoat generation regarding many, if not all, of these employee-driven changes. **Millennials have been blamed by older generations as being**

---

[2] DeSilver, Drew. "How the Workforce Changed since the Great Recession Began." *Pew Research Center*, Pew Research Center, 30 Nov. 2017, www.pewresearch.org/fact-tank/2017/11/30/5-ways-the-u-s-workforce-has-changed-a-decade-since-the-great-recession-began/.

disloyal, entitled, attached to their phones, self-absorbed, spoiled, affirmation-needy, and whiney. And that sad list is only the start of the bashing many of us have read about and witnessed firsthand from the millennial-haters.

Research shows that most Gen Xers (born 1949-1964) and baby boomers (born 1965-1979) want the same things as these "whiney" millennials (born 1980-1999). This fact is a key premise of this book. **Great leaders understand that employees want many of the same things, regardless of their age and generational grouping.**

Millennials came into the workforce fast and strong with "demands" for work-life balance, personal values mirrored by corporate values, the desire to make an impact at work, and wellness as a priority (not an add-on). Some of today's leaders were stunned and amazed by what these outspoken and not-yet-deserving young folks were requesting. Leaders told me that they feared that the new millennial workforce wanted special and unearned benefits from a working world they knew nothing about.

For whatever reason (different parenting, changes in education, or technology), the millennial generation has had little problem asking for (and getting) at the beginning of their careers exactly what the rest of the workforce has always wanted but was too timid to request.

Good People Come Prior to Good Policies

Sadly, many of the **human resource tools** used over the past 20+ years to manage our ever-changing workforce **have not changed**. (Disclaimer: There are a number of Fortune 100 Companies that have a history of prioritizing the needs of their workers, and these companies have made some great changes. There are also some great smaller, more nimble organizations that have their ears to the ground and want to create a working environment that meets the demands of today's workforce. We will try to learn from their helpful examples.)

The good news is that leaders, unlike managers, have never waited for the human resources department to initiate better practices to create meaningful changes that address the current needs of their people. In fact, effective leaders and their smart actions have always come prior to good policies, helpful forms, or an effective system.

Readers may want to consider making some practical and independent changes that will immediately impact how they are perceived as leaders and how their team members work together. To help with this objective, I've included at the end of each chapter a section that serves as both a chapter summary and a practical guide for introducing FRESH Leadership practices immediately.

There is so much to learn when it comes to becoming a great leader. There are plenty of great stories out there. However, the most critical advice related to leadership development is this: **to become the leader you were meant to be, you must use the natural strengths, talents, and insights that have led you to where you are at this moment**. Imitating another person's leadership style will only allow you to become a bad imitation of someone else.

The (close) second-most critical advice related to leadership is this: **strong teams can only be built by focusing on the strengths of the team members, not their deficiencies**. Great leaders foster individual growth, mutual appreciation, and connectedness among team members which leads to the result of the team's efforts being more valuable than the sum of the team members' contributions.

Despite my fascination with the leadership traits of Abraham Lincoln, I recognize that his success was the result of his ability to lead using the lessons of his humble life as his guide. He did not attempt to be the leader he was not. He was a self-educated farm boy from Illinois with few high-profile Washington connections and a largely unsuccessful political career prior to becoming the President of the United States.

Lincoln capitalized on the fact that he was someone who could connect with the everyday worker and voter. He chose to be called "The Rail-splitter" candidate to highlight, instead of erase, his working-class roots. Lincoln also knew that he needed to focus on the strengths of his talented former rivals, who were placed in his Cabinet soon after the inauguration. Never before had such an unharmonious group been thrust together.

Lincoln did not attempt to change them so much as he strove to harness what each of them did best. This meant something different was needed from each individual. From William H. Seward, who failed to attain the Republican presidential nomination, Lincoln needed to learn more about his ability to think futuristically—especially as it related to freeing slaves and welcoming Catholics into the US. From Salmon P. Chase, who also sought the Republican nomination, this meant using his financial expertise to ensure the country could withstand the financial burdens of the Civil War.

In these cases, and in many others, Lincoln did not focus on the potential weaknesses that each cabinet member might bring (strife, self-preoccupation, mutiny). Instead, he was determined to create a strong team because he knew the precise reason each member was exceptional in his own right.

Contained in this book are examples from many of the leaders I have worked with over the last few decades. These stories show the bumps in the road, and the small or large insights gained on their journey to becoming great leaders. It is these very personal highs and lows that have made them the leaders they are today. My hope for every reader is that they can uncover their own stories—from good and bad work experiences—that have shaped who they strive to be and how they want to be remembered as a leader.

The goal of this book is to take a hard look at where we are in the workplace today. What are the expectations of today's workers? Once we have a good idea of what's expected, we can evaluate how FRESH leadership practices—derived from both academic learning (book smarts) and real-life applications (street smarts)—can be implemented to grow and nurture a strong team. Finally, we will evaluate the broad and positive impact that FRESH leaders can make.

Shift to a Strengths-Based Perspective

One of the tools I will be referring to frequently within this book is the Clifton Strengths assessment. Prior to 2012, I was extremely skeptical of the many personality tools (e.g., DiSC, the Meyers-Briggs Type Indicator, the Predictive Index, the VIA Survey, and the Clifton Strengths assessment) that were being used by my clients in the early 2000s. In fact, I was dismayed by the unhealthy reliance many of my clients had on these tools.

In a nutshell, I considered these assessments to be invalid quizzes that allowed managers to put individuals in virtual personality boxes that would ultimately stunt their team members' growth and career aspirations.

I was familiar with many of these tools and had taken all of the abovenamed assessments, except one: the Clifton Strengths assessment. In July 2012, I broke down and purchased the book *StrengthsFinder*

2.0[3] by Tom Rath and Donald Clifton from my local Barnes and Noble bookstore.

I was shocked by its long-standing *New York Times* best seller rating (to date, it's one of the longest nonfiction best sellers of all time) and needed to educate myself firsthand about the organizational behavior flaws that I was sure it had.[4] I quickly scanned the book's contents and flipped to the book's last page. There, I found a sealed envelope that, once opened, contained the website and a code (to be used only once) that would give me access to the Clifton Strengths assessment.

The assessment took a bit longer than I expected, about 35 minutes. I received my results immediately and was initially put off and surprised by the findings. My "Top 5" strengths—Competition, Maximizer, Achiever, Activator, Significance—were not what I expected and certainly did not fit the descriptors I would have used to explain my personality or my strengths.

When I did more than merely scan my overall results, I was amazed and a bit embarrassed by how on-target my results were. The short report, entitled "My Signature Themes," was embarrassing because it forced me to admit that I might think a certain way, but I did not openly describe myself to others in the way that the Gallup report had.

I was most concerned by the strengths in the first and fifth positions, Competition and Significance. I considered competitive women to be annoying, pushy, and friendless. Competitive was a word I associated with stellar athletes and cutthroat executives, and I was neither.

---

[3] Rath, Tom. *StrengthsFinder* 2.0. Gallup Press, 2007.

[4] Kopf, Dan. "Only One Book Has Made the Amazon Top 10 Every Year for the Past Decade." *Quartz*, Quartz, 21 Dec. 2016, qz.com/868736/strengthfinder-2-0-is-the-only-book-that-has-made-the-amazon-top-ten-every-year-for-the-last-decade/.

Significance was also a stumbling block for me. It was mortifying to think that I might be someone who needed to be important in the eyes of others, Gallup's short definition of Significance. I could tolerate and even accept the three other terms in my "Top 5" (Maximizer, Achiever, and Activator) but these two "strengths"—Competition and Significance—were, from my perspective, embarrassing personality flaws at best and detrimental character weaknesses at worst.

It took me some time to understand that these five terms described in my report were positive traits and, if used properly, could allow me to reach greater success and personal fulfillment. Despite my initial concern and confusion about what the terms meant, and only after reading my report multiple times, I found that the Clifton Strengths report allowed me to see myself more clearly and more honestly.

Unlike other personality assessments I was familiar with, the Clifton Strengths results were significantly more specific and less generalized. They did not predict a specific career path but encouraged me to evaluate a number of activities rather than occupations. And they did not focus on the negative aspects of my personality traits.

I appreciated all of these factors, mostly because it increased the tool's face validity. Face validity is not a scientifically focused term, but rather a term that is connected to logic. For example, an IQ test has face validity if its results show that a student with high grades and terrific test results also scores well on the IQ test. From my perspective, the Clifton Strengths did a good job of convincing me that it could predict what it claimed it can predict: my strengths.

In December 2013, I was among the first seven people in the world to receive training to become a Gallup Certified Strengths Coach. I had come full circle from being an assessment skeptic to an assessment pusher. The Clifton Strengths assessment is a tool that also mirrors my desire to combine both book smarts and street smarts. The Clifton

Strengths assessment was developed after over 25 years of psychology research and testing of reliability and validity (book smarts), and the written reports have actionable insights that can be used by leaders to develop and engage employees (street smarts).

Today, I help many small (100+ employee) and large (30,000+ employee) organizations develop great leaders who can, in turn, grow high performing teams. Understanding one's strengths and one's teammates' strengths is the first step I initiate with my clients who want to enhance their leadership skills. Importantly, the Clifton Strengths assessment is not the **only** tool that can be used in combination with the FRESH leadership techniques presented in this book, but it is the tool that I prefer and recommend.

More than ever before, today's leaders need to connect with their team members on a personal basis, using a developmental and supportive approach. I recommend leaders focus on the best abilities—or the strengths—of their team, not their weaknesses and deficiencies. Such a focus will build a group that feels valued and understood by both their leader and by their fellow team members.

The Framework

This book is written for anyone who is curious about leadership and teamwork. It is also written for those who may be concerned that today's leadership practices are out of sync with today's worker.

In an effort to appeal to (and hopefully appease) both of these readers, this book has been organized into three sections. I've also included at the end of each chapter a section entitled "Turning New Knowledge into Results" which I hope will serve both as a review of sorts as well as a jump-start for those who want to make real life changes.

There is so much information at our fingertips and an almost limitless potential to gain new insights about the issues that interest us. However, learning is not the same as doing. Changing long-held behaviors can be difficult to initiate and even more challenging to maintain.

The questions posed within these end-of-chapter sections are meant to serve as a probing guide for both leaders and team members. The headings under this final section are entitled Leader Self-Examination Questions and Group Discussion Questions. I highly encourage leaders and teams to use this book as a tool to initiate candid conversations about values, expectations, blind spots, vulnerability, meaningful work, development, and so much more. Ideally, these questions can illuminate the way for leaders and teams who want to find a fresh path to success.

Section One

This section (chapters 1 and 2) addresses the problems leaders currently face and considers how the playing field has changed, for better or for worse, over the course of history (but especially in the last two decades). Without a doubt, these changes make leadership more challenging today than ever before.

Chapter 1 presents research that helps us determine what works and what doesn't. "Why fix what ain't broke?" Right? Unfortunately, there are some real issues of brokenness in today's workforce that are a direct result of leaders who have not responded to the demands of today's environment.

Chapter 2 assesses how our expectations of work have changed. Some of these shifts are due to sociological changes (norms and values have evolved over time), and some are due to organizational changes (the type of work and how it gets performed).

Section Two

This section (chapters 3, 4, 5, 6, and 7) looks at each of the terms that make up the acronym F.R.E.S.H.: Feedback, Rewards, Engagement, Service, Human Connection.

These five chapters will illuminate how leaders can use their history, values, and life experiences to become an authentic leader and a source of inspiration for each team member.

Section Three

The final section (chapters 8, 9 and 10) examines how leadership and life are intertwined. Chapter 8 presents compelling evidence to show why leaders need candid feedback from trusted colleagues to lead effectively. Chapter 9 addresses how lifetime learning, self-improvement, and growth are not optional activities for leaders—they are necessities.

Lastly, we will consider how being a FRESH leader is neither easy or linear, but developing the skills presented in *FRESH Leadership* will positively impact every area of a leader's life.

SECTION ONE

Chapter One
MIND THE GAP

To win in the marketplace you must first win in the workplace.
– Doug Conant, Former CEO of Campbell's Soup

Those who have traveled to London and have used its public subway system (affectionately nicknamed the Tube) are likely to be familiar with the phrase "Mind the gap." It is impossible to miss the audible and visual warnings that pepper the commuters' ears and eyes. The messages are well-intended—the London Underground does not want its travelers to fall onto the train tracks when crossing the gap between the train door and the station platform.

This chapter evaluates a different kind of gap—but a gap that is similar in that it can have dire consequences if ignored. One might think that because the current US economy is strong and unemployment low that employees are happy with their leaders and inspired to work hard for them. Unfortunately, that optimistic idea has been shown to be incorrect by multiple sources. Below are three reports that indicate where the gaps reside.

Harvard Business Review (2018) presents the following research that squashes the positive notion that leaders are motivational:

- **65% of employees would *forgo* a pay raise if it meant seeing their boss *fired*.**
- **82% of employees see their leader as fundamentally *uninspiring*.**

This same *Harvard Business Review* article presents discouraging research indicating that leaders have a fundamental lack of perspective when judging their own leadership abilities. Despite the employee statistics noted above, this research found that **76% of leaders rate themselves as inspiring and motivating.**[5]

Results from John Templeton Foundation's Gratitude Survey (2012) found that:

- **81% of employees said they would work harder for a boss who appreciated them.**
- **70% of employees said they'd feel better about their work and themselves if their boss thanked them more regularly.**[6]

Another study, discussed in an October 2018 *Inc.* magazine article, reported that:

- **32% of workers report meaningful work to be more important than compensation.**[7]

---

[5] Brewerton, Rasmus HougaardJacqueline CarterVince, and Harvard Business Review. "Why Do So Many Managers Forget They're Human Beings?" *Harvard Business Review*, 5 Feb. 2018, hbr.org/2018/01/why-do-so-many-managers-forget-theyre-human-beings.

[6] "Gratitude Revealed." *John Templeton Foundation*, www.templeton.org/grant/gratitude-revealed.

[7] Mikel, Betsy. "Science Finds You'd Take a 32 Percent Pay Cut If Your New Job Offered This Instead." *Inc.com*, Inc., 3 Oct. 2017, www.inc.com/betsy-mikel/1-compelling-reason-why-youd-take-a-job-that-paid-32-percent-less-science-finds.html.

To better understand the meaning of this recent and relevant research, let's dissect and examine the findings presented.

The research presented in the *Harvard Business Review* shows a large and concerning disconnect between how leaders rate themselves and how they are rated by their staff. Leaders, like all human beings, are susceptible to self-rater bias.[8]

Over-inflating our own abilities is a common phenomenon. For example, multiple studies have found that most drivers believe they are better and safer on the roads than the average driver. This same bias occurs for leaders who believe they are doing a good job when it comes to inspiring their troops.

The sobering research presented by the *Harvard Business Review* indicates that, on average, a leader who currently manages 10 people has fewer than four team members who find him or her to be tolerable as a boss. In fact, the majority of this team of 10 people would give up pay to have that boss leave and never return. These results are enough to make any leader squeamish.

The research presented by John Templeton's Foundation mirrors these results but focuses on the level of appreciation felt by employees from their leaders. Again, the results show that about **three-fourths of employees would work harder and feel better if they were given more appreciation**. Frequently, studies such as these focus on the need for monetary incentives as a means to thank employees. Importantly, this data focuses on verbal motivators that are as simple as saying "thank you."

---

[8] Brewerton, Rasmus HougaardJacqueline CarterVince, and *Harvard Business Review*. "Why Do So Many Managers Forget They're Human Beings?" Harvard Business Review, 5 Feb. 2018, hbr.org/2018/01/why-do-so-many-managers-forget-theyre-human-beings.

Finally, the WorkHuman Research Institute's research examines the desire for meaningful work. In this study, comprising 2,700 U.S. workers, meaningful work was ranked first in importance, while compensation was ranked third.[9]

Of course, workers having an interest in meaningful work is not new. There is a well-known and oft-referenced story about a NASA janitor who, in 1961, upon meeting President John F. Kennedy, was asked by the President what he did at NASA. The worker replied, "I'm helping put a man on the moon." Remarkably, the janitor's response transcended the physical tasks of his job and emphasized the meaning behind the work he was accomplishing. Research consistently emphasizes the importance of meaningful work and links meaningful work with better health, wellbeing, teamwork, and engagement.

Today, more than ever before, workers want to know their work has a purpose that is greater than increasing organizational profits. Unfortunately, too many workers do not believe their work has meaning. The results from a 12,000-employee survey by the Energy Project found that as many as 50% of workers, from a wide range of industries, believe that they do not have meaningful work.[10]

This same study found that those who find their jobs meaningful are three times as likely to stay with their organization. **Having meaningful work was *the most important factor* to workers staying with a job**, even when compared with highly sought factors such as learning and growth, connection to the company's missions, and work-life balance.

---

[9] Bolden-Barrett, Valerie. "Meaningful Work Is Critical to Worker Happiness, Study Says." HR Dive. October 10, 2017. Accessed January 28, 2019. https://www.hrdive.com/news/meaningful-work-is-critical-to-worker-happiness-study-says/506877/.

[10] "Why You Hate Work." The Energy Project. June 19, 2018. Accessed January 28, 2019. https://theenergyproject.com/why-you-hate-work-2/.

In summary, many in today's workforce are looking for leaders who can provide these three things:
1. Inspiration and motivation
2. Genuine appreciation for the work they do
3. A connection to the meaning behind the work they are doing

Addressing the Gap

Leaders need to rise to the occasion and close this gap between how they think they are performing and how employees perceive them. Today's workforce needs a new kind of leader who is less of an emotionally-devoid Vulcan and more of an attuned and emotionally intelligent colleague—someone who can motivate employees by looking at the big picture, who can praise employees and understand their contribution to the daily grind, who can connect the dots for employees, and who can show them that their work is important and meaningful.

In the past, leaders may have attempted to learn the ropes of leadership by mimicking their past leaders' actions or techniques. The research presented here shows that such efforts are insufficient. Employees expect more from their leaders and from the work itself.

Unwritten Rules and Unwritten Needs

Most workers realize that the most important "rules" at work are the unwritten rules. Organizational psychologists call the process of understanding these rules at work "socialization"—it is the method by which employees come to learn the culture of the organization.

The socialization process occurs when we go to work and see what other people (especially leaders) do, pay attention to, and say. From this socialization process, we gather information and create a personal list of unwritten rules, some of which may apply **only** to our immediate boss, but by which we schedule our work lives and routines.

Most workers also have unwritten *needs* that are separate from the organization's rules. These needs help us decide if the organization we are working for is a good match for us. In the past, it is the gap between workers' unwritten needs and the reality of the workplace that have given rise to unions, which represent workers' needs as a united front against employers. Today's employers—ever wary of unions—are more aware of workers' needs, but they continue to stumble over how to create a culture that simultaneously meets the organization's rules and the worker's needs.

Unfortunately, ineffective managers frequently operate using decades-old unwritten rules and are blind to the unwritten and extremely relevant needs of today's workers. Quite simply, the old rules that many seasoned executives live by and lead by are no longer relevant to the workforce they manage —but these same executives are slow to recognize the incompatibility of "how things used to run around here" and the realities of the modern workforce.

Old Work Rules and New Work Needs

On the next page are two lists that provide examples of the unwritten work *rules* of the past and the unwritten work *needs* of the present. The Unwritten Work Rules of the Past list summarizes the old-school way of thinking that pervaded the workplace over the past few decades.

The list depicts what employers wanted from employees, what was valued in the workplace, and how things operated on a daily basis, regardless of what the written rules in the corporate handbook might indicate. Some managers believe these rules are still okay. These stuck-in-1993 managers will never become true leaders because they cling to the underlying belief that these rules worked well "in the good ol' days" and could work today, if people would just stop complaining.

The Unwritten Work Rules of the Past

- The "come in before the boss and leave after the boss" rule dictates your working hours if you plan to get ahead.
- Work is not meant to be fun. That's why they call it work.
- A "Type A" personality is best. People who show ambition, aggression, competitiveness, drive, impatience, need for control, and a sense of urgency in all things are praised and on the fast track.
- Masculinity and leadership are synonyms.
- Diversity is aspired to but rarely achieved.
- Skipping lunch or quickly grabbing something is best. Being so busy that lunch is "forgotten" gives you bragging rights.
- Leaders are strong and invisible.
- Weaknesses and emotions are hidden at all costs.
- Illness (especially serious illness) is almost viewed like leprosy—it is both pitied and feared.
- Work is not for socializing; close friendships decrease productivity.
- No news is good news. Don't expect to get a lot of feedback if things are going well. However, you'll get an earful if things are going poorly.

The Unwritten Work Needs of the Present list summarizes a new way of thinking about work and how to get it done. The list is written from the perspective of the modern employee and depicts what employees currently want from an employer, what they value in the workplace, and how things should ideally operate in their workplace. Some of the needs listed may be standard operating procedure at your organization. Others may be alluded to—for example the need for increased feedback about performance—but not proactively addressed.

The Unwritten Work Needs of the Present

- "Facetime" in the office is less important than maintaining meaningful connections—during normal working hours and after.
- Work is a central part of life and should add meaning and enjoyment.
- There is no perfect personality type at work. A successful team needs a balance of different personalities—some hard charging, and some laid back.
- Openness, collective thinking, and historically "feminine" traits are considered necessary leadership characteristics.
- Diversity is imperative.
- Socializing at work is encouraged—as is having a best friend at work.
- Strengths are emphasized. Weaknesses are discussed and managed around.
- Putting words to our emotions and helping others do the same strengthens connections between team members.
- Leaders are human beings with vulnerabilities. Real leaders are emotionally astute.

- Illness is understood, and support is given to those in need.
- Feedback is essential. No news is NOT good news. Positive feedback allows individuals to improve upon past successes. Negative feedback provides the opportunity to learn and grow from less-than-perfect outcomes.

Leaders, as opposed to managers, are aware of and sympathetic to the needs of their employees and can create a team environment that meets these needs. Too often, old school managers stick their heads in the sand, try to live by the old rules, and attempt to ignore or diminish the current needs of employees.

Managing like this is akin to using a decades-old computer instead of upgrading to a newer, faster, more efficient version. These individuals can still get some things done … but not at the pace or quality that would make them great. This sad reality is the genesis of this book.

There is a gap. This gap has grown like a small tear in a sweater that at first looks harmless and is barely noticeable. Slowly, it gets bigger. What had seemed to be just a snag has now become an enormous, gaping hole. The gap between what employees need and what managers provide is similar to the tear in the sweater. It is an obvious hole that grew over time, and in some cases, it is vast. But it can be repaired. The repair will transform the manager into a leader.

We've learned that frequently these gaps exist because there is a difference between a manager's desired reality and the employees' actual realities. They may be a result of the employees' perception of their leaders' abilities, how appreciated the employees feel, how meaningful their work is, or how fully their unspoken needs are being met. Without investigation and measurement, it is impossible for anyone to predict the exact cause and how big their organizations' gaps might be.

There are number of tools that claim to quantify such organizational questions. For example, 360-degree surveys assess a leader's abilities, satisfaction surveys measure the contentment of employees, and employee engagement surveys examine how valued and involved employees feel at work.

Knowledge is power, and some experts suggest that all of these tools should be used annually to quantify where an organization may be falling short. I encourage the decision-makers within an organization to introduce only one of these measurement tools—Gallup's engagement assessment tool, known as the Q12. As will be discussed in greater depth in chapter 5, this 12-item assessment of employee engagement can appraise all of these issues simultaneously.

Summary

This chapter examined the disconnect between managers' perceptions and employees' work realities and encourages managers who want to be leaders to be mindful of these gaps. Managers, who are uninspiring, lacking in appreciation of their staff's contributions and unwilling to help their team find meaning in their work, may be at risk of falling into the oncoming train traffic. Importantly, these managers will fall short of what it takes to be a true leader. Chapter 2 will evaluate how our expectations—for work and for life—have changed.

Turning New Knowledge into Results

To prepare yourself and your team to move forward in a FRESH way, consider the questions on the next page. The first set of questions, under the heading Leader Self-Examination Questions, are meant to spark introspection, while the second set of questions, under the heading Group Discussion Questions, may be used to prompt an informal group discussion of the issues presented in chapter 1.

Leader Self-Examination Questions

1. What are your unwritten rules at work? Where did you learn these rules (parents, teachers, first boss, best/worst boss)?
2. Do your team members have their own unwritten work rules? Can you guess what some of their rules might be? Honestly assess your feelings related to the needs of your employees. Are you able to respond to their workplace needs?
3. On a scale of 1 to 5 (with 1 being terrible and 5 being fantastic), how would you rate yourself—being brutally honest—on your ability to:
   - Inspire and motivate staff
   - Appreciate the work they do
   - Communicate an appreciation of their work
   - Create a connection to the meaning behind the work they are doing.
4. Has your organization measured the engagement of staff in the past? If so, what actions were taken to increase engagement? If not, why is employee engagement an area of inaction?

Group Discussion Questions

1. Does our organization have any old-school rules that live on or at least linger around?
2. What is your number one, most important, workplace need?

3. How could we do a better job to motivate staff, show appreciation, communicate thanks, and connect our work to meaning?
4. What is the best part of your job? Why?
5. How can we work together to have more time every week doing our favorite things at work?

Chapter Two

TODAY'S EXPECTATIONS

High expectations are the key to everything.
– Sam Walton, founder of Walmart, the world's largest employer

Expectations Have Changed

Expectations of work have changed over time. There are an array of new questions that we ponder: Is my job meaningful? Is work just a paycheck? Is my job a symbol to the world of who I am and what I value? Is this the job I am meant to be doing? These questions tap into sociological issues regarding the norms in our society.

Our work expectations have changed at a similar rate and in a similar way to our changing expectations about marriage. I was talking to a retired publishing executive when these similarities first occurred to me. The retired executive, Tom, was sharing his wife's discontent with her role as an editor for a well-regarded publisher. Tom summarized his wife's difficulties by saying, "If this job were a marriage, she'd be long gone." I was struck by his candor.

Much like the way our culture currently has high expectations of what a successful and happy marriage looks like, our culture also has high expectations of work. Consider being an American a century ago: marriage and work were both considered necessities that were not expected to be filled with joy and fulfillment. They were just part of a mature adult's duty. The common wisdom and cultural pressures of the time encouraged individuals to stay loyal to their spouse and job, even if things were less than ideal. In sum, the goal was not necessarily to be highly engaged with one's spouse or job, but to be steadfastly dedicated to them.

Although divorce rates in the United States have been declining in recent years, research continues to show that between 40 and 50 percent of married couples in the US will divorce. And those who marry again are at higher risk for divorce. Our current rate of divorce is dramatically different from the past. The Census Bureau shows that from 1901-1915, the divorce rate ranged from 8%-15%, and in 1985, the divorce rate peaked at 50%.[11]

There are two commonly cited reasons for this increase in divorce rate over the last 100 years. The first relates to the increases in earning power of women during this timeframe, and, therefore, their decreased dependence upon men. Women's likelihood of attending college and pursuing jobs in higher paying professions has changed dramatically during this time. The second reason noted for the increase in divorce is the lack of stigma attached to divorce today as compared to a century ago.

Similarly, in the early 1900s the idea of climbing the corporate ladder—growing within an organization over time, getting promotions that were commensurate with your tenure, and being valued for your

---

[11] US Census Bureau. "Search Results." *Census Bureau QuickFacts,* United States Census Bureau, 13 Dec. 2014, www.census.gov/content/census/en/search-results.html?stateGeo=none&q=group+quarters&searchtype=web&page=3.

length of service—was akin to the American dream. More recently, *Fast Company* reports that workers are less likely to stay at one organization for their entire career, and some career experts recommend that individuals should switch jobs every three years to stay engaged and to keep growing.[12]

Our expectations of marriage and work have shifted over time. We have higher expectations and seek fulfillment in both and will leave our mate or our organization if our needs are not met. This makes the issue of engagement even more imperative. Whereas once an employee might stay at a job for years—or even an entire lifetime—despite low fulfillment and disengagement, today's employee is encouraged by friends, headhunters, the media, and job experts to make a move when their needs are not met.

Healthy organizations typically have a low turnover rate. However, some well-regarded and high-profit organizations, like Google and Amazon, are plagued by high turnover.

Within Fortune 500 companies in 2013, Google had the fourth highest employee turnover and Amazon was rated second.[13] Silicon Valley is well known for giving its employees fantastic benefits—like free food and on-site dry-cleaning services—but these benefits do not equate to low turnover rates. The demand for high-tech experts makes turnover a particularly difficult issue in this industry. Similarly, Uber's average employee tenure is just 1.8 years, Tesla comes in at 2.1 years, and even the highly regarded Facebook has a surprisingly brief average tenure of 2.5 years.

---

[12] Giang, Vivian. "You Should Plan On Switching Jobs Every Three Years For The Rest Of Your Life." *Fast Company*, Fast Company, 28 Dec. 2016, www.fastcompany.com/3055035/you-should-plan-on-switching-jobs-every-three-years-for-the-rest-of-your-

[13] Johnson, Tim. "The Real Problem With Tech Professionals: High Turnover." *Forbes*, Forbes Magazine, 29 June 2018, www.forbes.com/sites/forbesbusinessdevelopmentcouncil/2018/06/29/the-real-problem-with-tech-professionals-high-turnover/.

Turnover, morale, and engagement are intertwined issues. It is common to see turnover rise when morale and engagement are low. Of course, this correlation does not prove causation, but the relationship is clear. Even a small uptick in turnover can directly impact a team's morale and engagement.

I once worked with a team that had significant morale issues. The team's employee engagement scores were notably lower than the large organization's norm, most likely because four leaders had left the team within five years. After coaching the team members individually and as a group for a few months, I came to learn that a number of the team members were dissatisfied with their new boss and were also planning their exits. Soon thereafter, the leader confided in me that she was uncertain about her role. She, too, might abandon ship.

After eighteen months of tumultuous change, the team appeared to be approaching stability. The leader decided not to leave the organization, but her team had changed dramatically in the one and one-half years since I started working with them.

All but one of the original six team members had transferred to different departments within the organization or had left the organization completely. In a meeting with Kara, the self-described "last woman standing," I could see and hear her distress at being "stuck" in her role, unable to find a new job, and abandoned by her past workmates.

In this instance, workplace loyalty and seniority were far from Kara's mind. During our discussion, Kara made it clear that despite feeling undervalued in her current role, she was too intimidated by the unknown to make a wholehearted effort to leave her job. Unfortunately, this fact caused her to have doubts about her abilities. How was it that she could not accomplish what all of her peers could? More importantly, how could her friends—especially her best friend at work—leave her?

Kara's example brings up another workplace expectation that has changed over time—the expectation of having friends at work. Over the last two decades, the need for friends at work has increased. This need is almost certainly due to three issues related to **current workplace trends**: 1) our work hours have increased, 2) our connections to the community have decreased, and 3) our belief system about work has changed; work should be more than a paycheck.[14]

Friendship Expectations

Among the most controversial questions Gallup has asked in its 30+ years of engagement research is, "Do you have a best friend at work?" While some think this question is fairly straightforward, others (me included, initially) believe it to be either a non-relevant issue or a question that taps into what could be detrimental to a productive workplace. The "old work rules" say friendships and too much socializing can negatively impact productivity. As noted in the introduction, the "new work needs" of employees say that work should be more of an extension of oneself—including the self that is a social being.

Over the last five years, I've changed my opinion about the relevance of having a best friend at work. My stance has flip-flopped after noticing firsthand how critical friendships are to workplace morale and after taking to heart Gallup's engagement research. Gallup's composite engagement results (pooled from thousands of organizations) show that having a best friend at work is good for organizational engagement.

---

[14] Putnam, Robert D. *Bowling Alone: the Collapse and Revival of American Community*. Simon & Schuster, 2007.

Gallup's book, *Wellbeing: The Five Essential Elements,* presents information from Gallup's global study of the well-being found in more than 150 countries. The results dispute the idea that friendships negatively impact productivity. In fact, the study shows that **those with a best friend at work were seven times more likely to be engaged at their jobs than the respondents who did not report having a best friend**. Even more importantly, those **who didn't have a best friend or strong relationships at work only had a 1 in 12 chance of being engaged**.[15]

Some may wonder, how does having a best friend in the workplace translate into measurable productivity and increased performance? Gallup has found that if an organization can move the needle on the best friend ratio, there are clear and positive business outcomes. For instance, today only two out of ten US employees strongly agree that they have a best friend at work. However, if that ratio could be increased to six out of ten employees agreeing, organizations could achieve following outcomes:[16]

1. 36% fewer safety incidents
2. 7% more engaged customers
3. 12% higher profits

The old way of thinking asserts that work is not enjoyable and should be devoid of emotion. Yesterday's work was supposed to be a grind. Employees' new way of thinking is that work should be a means to participate in something bigger than themselves and it can foster meaningful relationships.

---

[15] Rath, Tom, and James K. Harter. *Wellbeing: the Five Essential Elements.* Gallup Press, 2014.

[16] Gallup, Inc. "Why We Need Best Friends at Work." *Gallup.com,* 15 Jan. 2018, www.gallup.com/workplace/236213/why-need-best-friends-work.aspx.

In sum, today's work can and should bring meaning and purpose to one's life. Today's leaders can be a central component of that, promoting the formation of meaningful friendships by creating teams that are built on trust, diversity, an appreciation for hard work, and mutual respect.

Teamwork Expectations

Teamwork, as opposed to independent work, has increased dramatically in the last two decades. **Some calculate the average time spent working with others has increased 50% or more in the last 20 years.**[17]

Many times, the result of the team's collaborative effort is greater than the sum of each individual's contribution. This is the magic of teamwork. But occasionally the teamwork doesn't work.

Most leaders are quick to identify those on their team who work most effectively with others and which team members work better when alone. Great leaders differ from average leaders because they are skilled at considering how their actions—as a leader—impact the team's overall performance.

High-performing leaders who produce strong teams are less likely to place blame on individual team members and more likely to recognize how their leadership is lacking when there are difficulties, when deadlines are missed, or when customers are disappointed. One of the key outcomes that top leaders have in common is their ability to create an ecosystem where teamwork can thrive.

Some of the most important elements that are needed in such an ecosystem are trust, diversity, an appreciation of hard work, and mutual respect. Below are examples of how leaders can successfully create productive environments with these four basic elements.

---

[17] Grant, Rob CrossReb RebeleAdam, et al. "Collaborative Overload." *Harvard Business Review*, 20 Dec. 2016, hbr.org/2016/01/collaborative-overload.

Create a Trusting and Fair Environment

Trust is the foundation of good leadership and strong teamwork. Being fair and trustworthy is a leader's first order of business. Squashing attempts by team members to create an unhealthy work environment—an environment of backstabbing, cynicism, cliques, or one-upping—is the second most important order of business. High performing leaders are good at detecting early signs of such behaviors and nipping them in the bud.

33% of employees said a lack of open, honest communication has the most negative impact on employee morale.[18]

Some leaders encourage "stabbing them in the heart, not the back" which translates into "tell a team member directly and to their face when you are put out or peeved with their behavior instead of telling another teammate about it behind someone's back."

Some might think such language is too harsh for the workplace, and I might agree. But regardless of the specific wording, the message from the leader—communicated by words and actions—needs to be "our team behaves in ways that promote trust and fairness." In chapter 3, we will discuss how a leader's receptivity to different opinions and to feedback from the team also impacts trust.

Value Diversity

Diversity can come in many forms: sex, race, religion, national origin, sexual orientation, weight, disability … the list goes on.

---

[18] Gadd, Michael. "Poor Communication Hurts Morale - Leadership Strategies - Communication." *Inc.com*, Inc., 6 Nov. 2008, www.inc.com/news/articles/2008/11/communication.html.

67% of job seekers say they look at whether a company is diverse when job hunting.[19]

Today, we recognize that there are different types of diversity (both visible and invisible), and that diversity improves teamwork. However, 20 years ago, the opposite belief was held. Most leaders I worked with early in my career believed that diversity referred to visible traits, that too much diversity could cause problems on a team, and any differences among team members was cause for diversity training.

For example, two decades ago, I worked with a sales team that was known for having and building great relationships with their customers. Common wisdom of that time declared this team needed more salespeople who were very similar to the current team members, if the team was to perform at that same high level.

A DIVERSE team can outperform a top performing, homogenous group by up to 58%.[20]

Most leaders today recognize that this "homogeneous is best" attitude is flawed. However, leaders can be slow to recognize how they may be inadvertently devaluing diversity. I recommend that leaders take a good look at the types of individuals they favor, count as key team players, and are genuinely impressed by. Leaders who value diversity surround themselves with, and take advice from, people who have a variety of personalities, abilities, and strengths—in sum people who are not like themselves.

The teams led by such leaders have fewer blind spots and greater success, as will be discussed in chapter 8. Leaders who overlook the

---

[19] Team, Glassdoor. "What Job Seekers Really Think of Your Diversity Stats|What Job Seekers Really Think of Your Diversity Stats." *Glassdoor,* 21 Dec. 2018, www.glassdoor.com/employers/blog/diversity/.

[20] Grant, David RockHeidi. "Why Diverse Teams Are Smarter." *Harvard Business Review,* 4 Nov. 2016, hbr.org/2016/11/why-diverse-teams-are-smarter.

benefits of diversity and surround themselves with people who look, act, or think just like themselves, create teams that have a one-sided, myopic vision of the world and its problems. Studies show that these less diverse teams do not perform as well as diverse teams.

Appreciate Hard Work

Having a team of hard workers is the opposite of having a team of social loafers. Social loafing occurs when individuals put forth less effort when working in a team than they would when working alone. In high school and college, instructors use feedback tools to assess the social loafing that can occur during a group project. Such tools are less prevalent in the workplace despite the fact that social loafing at work creates bad feelings, stress, and negativity among team members.

It is a leader's duty to be on the lookout for social loafing. It is the leader, not the individuals on the team, who should be preoccupied with the distribution of work among team members. When low performance by a team member is noted, both the leader and the team member in question should discuss the situation. Finding new ways for the underutilized team member to contribute to the overall goals of the team should be a priority.

67% of employees believe their colleagues can encourage/help them do their jobs better.[21]

An appreciation for hard work can be cultivated naturally when all team members feel utilized and are contributing their specialties at work. Leaders who understand the special talents of each team member can assign tasks and then follow up by giving each team member specific feedback and rewards related to their abilities on that task (see chapters 3 and 4). Finally, team members who are appreciated by their leader are more apt to feel secure in their position and appreciative of their colleagues.

---

[21] Lupfer, Elizabeth. "Social Knows: Employee Engagement Statistics (August 2011 Edition)." *The Social Workplace*, 8 Aug. 2011, thesocialworkplace.com/2011/08/social-knows-employee-engagement-statistics-august-2011-edition/.

Foster Mutual Respect During Communication

Successful teams have a track record of taking turns talking and giving equal time to each team member to communicate their opinion. In fact, research conducted by tech-giant Google has shown that **mutual respect during team communication (noted by everyone taking turns when talking and speaking for roughly the same amount of time) is one of two imperatives for team effectiveness.** (The other imperative discovered by Google's Project Aristotle, assessing over 180 teams from all over the company, is referred to as "average social sensitivity" or what I'll call group emotional intelligence in chapter 7.[22])

Participating on a team where one person monopolizes the discussion and plows forward with her ideas, obliterating any rival suggestions, can be exhausting and even enraging.

86% of employees and executives cite lack of collaboration or ineffective *communication* for workplace failures.[23]

Leaders who set clear communication ground rules when it comes to brainstorming, problem-solving, and figuring out a new strategy create an environment of open and safe communication (meaning no ideas are ridiculed). When team members recognize that everyone's viewpoint will be heard and considered, the need to be the loudest, longest, or most passionate communicator is lessened. Open and safe communication builds trust, just as trust builds open and safe communication.

---

[22] Schneider, Michael. "Google Spent 2 Years Studying 180 Teams. The Most Successful Ones Shared These 5 Traits." *Inc.com*, Inc., 19 July 2017, www.inc.com/michael-schneider/google-thought-they-knew-how-to-create-the-perfect.html.

[23] Arcari, Michael. "Press Release." *Work Faster!!! Urgency's Role in Performance Management - Fierce, Inc. - Fierce, Inc.*, Fierce, Inc., fierceinc.com/employees-cite-lack-of-collaboration-for-workplace-failures.

Meaningful Work Expectations

In chapter 1, a leader's ability to recognize his or her employees' desire to have meaningful work was presented as a potential gap. Research shows that people underestimate another person's need for intrinsic rewards (like meaningful work), despite recognizing how self-motivating intrinsic rewards are personally. The title of a 2017 *Harvard Business Review* article sums up this ironic issue—"Every Generation Wants Meaningful Work – But Thinks Other Age Groups Are in It for the Money."[24]

Believing that financial incentives and other extrinsic rewards (paid-for vacations, better benefit packages, or other tangible rewards) are the best or only way to motivate employees is an "old work rules" way to think. In chapter 4—Rewards, the need to reward employees in ways that tap into both intrinsic and extrinsic motivators will be discussed at length. Suffice it to say that employees of every age group are interested in meaningful work and leaders need to incorporate this new expectation into their understanding of motivation and engagement.

Summary

To summarize, chapter 2 reminds the reader to be aware of individual expectations at work. Going to work merely to receive a paycheck is quickly becoming a thing of the past. The responsibility of creating a workplace culture that breeds personal connections and emphasizes

---

[24] Pontefract, Dan, et al. "Every Generation Wants Meaningful Work - but Thinks Other Age Groups Are in It for the Money." *Harvard Business Review*, 31 July 2017, hbr.org/2017/07/every-generation-wants-meaningful-work-but-thinks-other-age-groups-are-in-it-for-the-money.

engagement is squarely on the shoulders of each team's leader. In the next chapter, we will see how giving and receiving meaningful and frequent feedback at work is the cornerstone of becoming a FRESH leader and creating this type of culture.

Turning New Knowledge into Results

Below are questions that can help you to uncover your work expectations as well as your team's expectations.

Leader Self-Examination Questions

1. What are your work expectations? Do you identify meaning and satisfaction from your role at work?
2. Under what circumstances would you leave your employer? What factor would be most persuasive to you: more money, more flexibility, more responsibility, less responsibility, better people, better products?
3. Do you have a best friend at work? Do you accept or reject the idea that friendships increase engagement and productivity? Do members of your team have close friendships?
4. Is your team consistently meeting your expectations of productivity? If not, why not?
5. Are there gaps between your desired levels and your team's actual levels of the following:
    - Trust
    - Diversity
    - Appreciation for hard work
    - Mutual respect

Group Discussion Questions

1. What do you think your parents' expectations of work were? What was the loudest message that they communicated to you about work?
   - "Work is hard! That's why they call it work!"
   - "Do what you love! You'll always be happy!"
   - "Always give your best. At work and at home."
   - "When I was your age, I had it much harder."
   - Other
2. How have your parents' expectations impacted your expectations about work?
3. If anything were possible on our team, which of the following would you like to see more of:
   - Trust
   - Diversity
   - Appreciation for hard work
   - Mutual respect
4. Do you have any suggestions for ways to make any of the above ideals realized?

SECTION TWO

F.R.E.S.H.

Chapter Three
F.R.E.S.H. FEEDBACK

*We all need people who will give us feedback.
That's how we improve.*

–Bill Gates, former chairman, CEO, Microsoft

How Do You Handle Feedback?

Defensive? Hurt? Appalled? Grateful? Appreciative? Humbled? Feedback can stir a host of emotions. Every manager desires feedback … because they are human. How managers internally digest and externally respond to that feedback will determine if they remain managers or if they go on to develop into true leaders. If a manager claims to want feedback, but rejects it, the team members will be the first to sense this disconnect from authentic leadership.

Leaders promote an environment that is accepting of feedback—both positive and negative. Accepting, and not deflecting, positive feedback with words like "Thank you" or "I really appreciate you saying that" are important phrases that leaders need to incorporate into their "go-to" response list. Similarly, acknowledging, and not rejecting, negative feedback with responses like "I am sorry to hear that you feel that way. I will give your comments much thought" or "I did not intend to ___ (make you feel that way, give that impression to the team, come off in that light, etc.)," but I am grateful for knowing your thoughts now" are key to constructing an environment that values feedback.

Leaders are given the opportunity and the challenge of instilling a spirit of growth in the team. Modeling the best practices—the practices you hope to see in your team members—when receiving positive as well as negative feedback is every leader's job. Openness and honesty are cultivated by leaders who praise team members for giving all types of feedback and who use that feedback to reconsider their perspective.

U.S. Schools Hardwire Our Need for Feedback

Feedback, in the form of grades, is a foundational part of the United States educational system. Grades are regularly doled out in primary schools across our country, as early as first grade. Competitive high schools and colleges pride themselves in creating challenging environments to prepare students for future jobs or more advanced degrees. The workload can seem ridiculous and extreme. However, I have come to appreciate our American educational system and its heavy emphasis on grades. Grades are an indisputable form of feedback.

For one semester, during my four-year college experience, I attended the University College London (UCL). It was a fantastic opportunity to live and learn in another country. However, there was an issue that ultimately undermined the entire learning experience: there was no feedback. None.

In the United Kingdom, it is not unusual to have a year-long class with no quizzes, papers, group projects, or tests until the end-of-year (not end-of semester!) exam. For some students, such a learning environment allows them to attend classes and soak up the information in a less pressured and test-focused environment.

For someone like me, who needs to know exactly how they are progressing at every minute, this environment incited anxiety and dread. My success as a student, prior to this experience, had been based on a time-tested formula of spending a good part of the semester figuring my teachers out, homing in on their preferences, and zeroing in on their testing habits.

My grades on all of the (less important) quizzes, presentations, and mid-terms prior to the end of the semester were benchmarks that helped me create a study plan for the all-important final exam. Without these sign-posts, prior to the cumulative final, I felt lost and confused, scared, and unsure. My grades were extremely important to me. In my mind, the goal was not merely to get an undergraduate degree. To feel proud of myself, I had to hit certain benchmarks. Accomplishing these goals was the job I had given myself, and I could not be persuaded by my friends who were less ambitious and grade-focused than I was that "it wasn't that big of a deal."

Ultimately, I left UCL after one semester, instead of spending a full year, because the lack of performance feedback was intolerable for me. I longed to know how I was doing in my classes … even if that meant receiving negative feedback. The silence from my UCL professors was deafening. I needed to return to my country and my college, where I would be inundated with papers, quizzes, tests, and mid-terms, and, importantly, the grades that came with those assignments. I craved feedback.

To some, this example might seem extreme or unrelated to the working world. Research shows otherwise.

Studies show that 65% of all employees want more feedback.[25]

Given the fact that US citizens are raised in a remarkably feedback-rich educational environment, it should not be surprising that more than six out of ten employees want more feedback at work. Some say feedback is the most important form of communication that occurs at work.

The book-smart definition of feedback is that it gives us information to discern how well we are meeting our goals. Street-smart leaders know that giving honest feedback helps people make better decisions, improves the work people do, and makes the leader more effective in the team's eyes.

Leaders who gave honest feedback were rated 5 times more effective than ones who did not.[26]

Leaders should not be shy about giving positive or negative feedback. Feedback of both types is a critical component of improving performance and engagement. We are most trusting of those who can give both positive and negative feedback because we recognize that people who do so are being honest.

Although it might be hard for some to believe that negative feedback can increase engagement, research shows this to be true. Even though negative feedback can injure our fragile egos, lead to worry about our job security, and make us wonder if our boss values our contributions, it proves that our boss is paying attention to us. **A 2009 Gallup poll**

---

[25] Lipman, Victor. "65% Of Employees Want More Feedback (So Why Don't They Get It?)." *Forbes*, Forbes Magazine, 9 Aug. 2016, www.forbes.com/sites/victorlipman/2016/08/08/65-of-employees-want-more-feedback-so-why-dont-they-get-it/.

[26] Folkman, Joseph. "The Best Gift Leaders Can Give: Honest Feedback." *Forbes*, Forbes Magazine, 19 Dec. 2013, www.forbes.com/sites/joefolkman/2013/12/19/the-best-gift-leaders-can-give-honest-feedback/.

found that employees who received negative feedback were 20 times more likely to be engaged than employees who received no feedback at all.[27]

Most workers thrive when given positive feedback because it can have the opposite effect of negative feedback. It can positively impact our egos, increase our sense of job security, and underscore our feelings of being valued. **Less surprising is the fact that employees who receive positive feedback are 30 times more likely to be engaged than those who received no feedback at all.**[28]

Effective Feedback

The obvious conclusion that can be drawn from this research is that feedback of ANY kind is important to improve work performance as well as engagement.

If we personalize the somewhat tricky issue of negative feedback and ask ourselves, "When am I most apt to accept negative feedback?" I think we would find that **we are *most able* to accept negative feedback from those we trust, and those who we believe, ultimately, value us**.

It is for this reason that I encourage leaders to build trust and increase the likelihood that employees feel valued by them. The easiest way to do this is to provide regular comments that specifically address the good works of employees (or in other words give regular and specific positive feedback). When a concern pops up, address the concern in the same prompt and direct manner (or in other words also give negative feedback).

---

[27] Gallup, Inc. "Driving Engagement by Focusing on Strengths." *Gallup.com*, 12 Nov. 2009, news.gallup.com/businessjournal/124214/driving-engagement-focusing-strengths.aspx

[28] Ibid.

On the next page are examples of various feedback methods and a summary of the effectiveness (or lack thereof) of each. The first are the BEAR and the BET methods of giving feedback. The BEAR method is used to give negative feedback and the BET method is used to deliver positive feedback. Both methods help leaders to deliver feedback that is clear and behaviorally focused.[29]

Everyone has heard the common advice "Don't just tell someone, 'Good job.' Instead, tell him what he is doing well and why you appreciate his actions." Generalized feedback like "Great job," or "That was not your best performance," does not help individuals to repeat the productive behaviors or discontinue the unhelpful behaviors. Leaders need to be specific and clear. The BEAR and BET methods help leaders keep their messages on point.

---

[29] Pauly, Jailza. "Positive Feedback Mechanisms: Promoting Better Communication Environm..." *LinkedIn SlideShare*, 11 Mar. 2016, www.slideshare.net/JailzaPauly/positive-feedback-mechanisms-promoting-better-communication-environments-in-research-groups.

BEAR EXAMPLE: NEGATIVE FEEDBACK

BEHAVIOR

During today's presentation, I noticed that you were writing an e-mail on your laptop for the first 15 minutes. After that, you deleted old e-mails until the presentation was completed.

EFFECT

I was frustrated by your behavior because we have discussed how working on our laptops during meeting time is distracting to the presenter and does not indicate a respect for your team members' ideas.

ALTERNATIVES

What are some ways you can focus your attention during our team meetings? I realize you are busy. Possibly you should leave your laptop and phone at your desk during our team meetings in the future to help you focus on the meeting's content.

RESULT

If you can eliminate your need to answer e-mails during our team meetings, that will improve the atmosphere in our meetings and increase the mutual respect felt by the team.

BET EXAMPLE: POSITIVE FEEDBACK

BEHAVIOR

In your presentation today, I noticed what a great job you did connecting to our client using non-technical terms that they could understand, making eye contact with them, and even using humor to lighten things up.

EFFECT

I was excited and impressed that you had improved upon the communication issues we discussed in our 1:1 meeting a few months ago. You did a great job addressing the gaps we discussed.

THANK YOU

Thank you! You are a hard worker and I appreciate all of your efforts.

No More Sandwich Method

Another common technique when delivering feedback is the Sandwich Method. This method has claimed its name because it encourages leaders to sandwich the negative feedback in between two positive feedback sentences. Years ago, it was believed that the sandwich method made negative feedback more palatable for the receiver. More recent discussions of this method claim that it can negatively impact the receiver in the following ways:

1. The receiver only hears the positive feedback. The negative feedback is diminished or metaphorically swept under the rug.
2. The receiver braces herself whenever positive feedback is given with the anticipation that negative feedback is on its way.
3. The receiver questions the feedback-giver's honesty.

Focus on Strengths

Teams that focus on what each member does best, receive feedback about how they are utilizing their strengths, and know how their unique talents connect to their work have higher productivity, increased profitability, and are six times more likely to be engaged at work.[30]

The leader sets the tone. They can create a strengths-based culture ("I'm so excited about the abilities of everyone here and the complementary skills of this team. We are unique. Let's use our unique talents to be the best we can be.") or a deficiency-based culture ("If only we were more like team B, they have some real stars. Let's do what they are doing."). Of course, research indicates that a strengths-based culture makes a team more productive, engaged, and satisfied. And, while harnessing the strengths of a team may sound challenging, it is a very straight-forward process that skilled leaders know is a vital component to creating a successful team.

---

[30] Gallup, Inc. "How Employees' Strengths Make Your Company Stronger." *Gallup.com*, 20 Feb. 2014, news.gallup.com/businessjournal/167462/employees-strengths-company-stronger.aspx.

One-quarter (25%) of American workers feel their strengths and weaknesses are "ignored" by their supervisors/managers, and 40% of these employees were actively disengaged.[31]

Some leaders are naturally gifted at understanding what each team member brings to the collective team effort that is unique and special. The rest of us need help to fully understand and appreciate the unique strengths of ourselves and others. Certainly, the one-quarter of supervisors and managers who are perceived by their direct reports to be ignoring the strengths and weaknesses of the team are in obvious need of help. Gallup's research shows that a leader who is unable to discuss an employee's capabilities (both good and bad) puts the engagement of the team at risk.

To date, about 20 million people worldwide have taken the Clifton Strengths assessment. Organizations like Google, Southwest Airlines, and Stryker (who are advocates for the Clifton Strengths assessment) are drawn to it because it takes the guess work out of knowing employees' strengths and weaknesses. Employees who take the Clifton Strengths assessment (and the leaders who learn their employees' results) can gain a powerful understanding of what they do best. Studies show that spending time working and learning in areas of our strength builds engagement.

Imagine being able to quickly grasp an overview of your team's innate abilities, while also deciphering its greatest area of weakness. Consider what it would be like to have something like a cheat sheet of each team member's strengths. Such a summary would help you to provide encouragement and training in the exact areas where each team member was most likely to blossom. How might this

---

[31] Gallup, Inc. "How Employees' Strengths Make Your Company Stronger." *Gallup.com*, 20 Feb. 2014, news.gallup.com/businessjournal/167462/employees-strengths-company-stronger.aspx.

impact you, each team member individually, and the team overall? At a bare minimum, learning each team member's Clifton Strengths assessment results would be an enormous advantage when doling out performance feedback.

The Dreaded Annual Review

Does your company have an annual review process? If your organization is like most, it continues to provide annual reviews for its employees. Despite the vast number of business articles with titles that are some variation on "The Annual Review Is Dead," the miserly annual review continues to be a common practice, and in some cases the **only** formal feedback mechanism, for organizations in the US and abroad.

26% of employees say their performance is evaluated less than once a year, while 48% say they are reviewed annually.[32]

Jack Welch, General Electric's CEO from 1981 to 2001, was well known for the cut-throat performance appraisals called stack ranking or forced ranking. This (now controversial) annual review process forces managers to place their direct reports into "buckets" and thereby group them according to ability.

The chosen ratio in each bucket might differ from company to company. An example would be allowing a manager to have 20% of employees in the top, 70% of employees in the middle, and 10% of employees in the bottom. The employees in the bottom bucket were at risk of being discharged (the worst-case scenario) or being placed on a performance improvement program (the best-case scenario).

---

[32] Gallup, Inc. "Give Performance Reviews That Actually Inspire Employees." *Gallup.com*, 25 Sept. 2017, www.gallup.com/workplace/236135/give-performance-reviews-actually-inspire-employees.aspx.

In 2015, GE did away with the stack ranking process because they realized it no longer suited the people working for them. Susan Peters, GE's head of human resources, stated in a *Quartz* article in August 2015, "I think some of it to be really honest is millennial based. It's the way millennials are used to working and getting feedback, which is more frequent, faster, mobile-enabled, so there were multiple drivers that said it's time to make this big change."[33]

As discussed in the Introduction, the millennial generation may be the scapegoat age group for GE's performance appraisal change, but research shows that the majority of all employees, not just millennials, want more frequent feedback. Organizations that have increased the amount of immediate and direct feedback given to employees are doing so to please employees as well as to meet the demands of their quickly changing businesses.

Many organizations haven't figured out what to do in lieu of an annual review process. One human resources vice president told me that she knew the process was lacking in usefulness for the 30,000+ employees that her organization oversaw. But she also realized that, for some, this once-a-year check-in was the only feedback they might receive, and therefore, she was deeply hesitant to do away with this less-than-stellar tool.

Only 26% of managers and employees think the traditional annual review process works, according to a survey of 169 North American companies.[34]

---

[33] Nisen, Max. "Why GE Had to Kill Its Annual Performance Reviews after More than Three Decades." *Quartz*, Quartz, 13 Aug. 2015, qz.com/428813/ge-performance-review-strategy-shift/.

[34] "Here's an Alternative to The Dreaded Annual Performance Review." *Fortune*, Fortune, fortune.com/2015/12/11/performance-review-alternative/.

Frequent Feedback Strategy

On the next page is a three-step method for giving performance feedback, called The Feedback Game Plan, that addresses many of the shortcomings of traditional annual reviews. This method incorporates the BEAR and BET methods. It can be used to document employee development or areas of concern and encourages employees to take control of their short- and long-term goals.

Performance-based discussions between a leader and an employee should drive improvements in the employee's work as well as document the history of the employee's work. While many leaders prefer spontaneous feedback, the need for a paper trail, in today's litigious world, cannot be overlooked.

Gallup found that when managers provide daily feedback (versus annual feedback) their employees were 3.6 times more likely to agree that they are motivated to do outstanding work.[35]

Having a plan for how and when to give feedback to team members should be like having an agenda before a big meeting: standard operating procedure. Unfortunately, some organizations confuse the need to create a thoughtful and routine feedback plan for leaders with the desire to have more formal communications between leaders and team members. This is a misconception. Research shows that it is the frequency—not the formality—of the process, that improves performance.

---

[35] Gallup, Inc. "Do Your Measures Make Employees Mad? Or Motivate Them?" *Gallup.com*, www.gallup.com/workplace/231659/performance-measures-motivate-madden-employees.aspx.

Feedback Game Plan

1. Communicate with staff members EVERY DAY about their performance. These brief interactions, that can occur verbally or using e-mail or texts, should be informal and signify that the leader cares about the team member's work. In *Unstuck at Last: Using Your Strengths to Get What You Want*, I discuss how anyone can become a leader by recognizing the strengths of others and commenting on those strengths.[36]

   Praise—at work or at home—triggers a release in dopamine, the famous neurotransmitter that helps moderate the pleasure and reward centers in our brain. Dopamine, an organic compound, helps us feel good at work and can also improve our innovative thinking and creative problem-solving. Unfortunately, we need regular supplies of dopamine. Jim Harter, chief scientist at the Gallup Organization, states that "recognition is a short-term need that has to be satisfied on an ongoing basis."[37]

2. Use the BEAR and BET methods **EVERY WEEK** to address and document good and poor performance. As noted previously, leaders need to create a paper trail that tells the full story of each team member's performance history. Leaders can use the BEAR and BET templates (found in appendix A) to record their notes, prompt their verbal discussions of performance, and add to the team member's file for future reference.

---

[36] Robinson, Sarah K. *Unstuck at Last: Using Your Strengths to Get What You Want*. United States: Sarah K. Robinson, 2015.

[37] Gallup, Inc. "In Praise of Praising Your Employees." *Gallup.com*, 9 Nov. 2006, www.gallup.com/workplace/236951/praise-praising-employees.aspx.

Ideally, the positive interactions (captured in writing using the BET method) will outnumber the BEAR-captured negative interactions by at least three-to-one. **Research has found that it takes three positive interactions to offset the negative impact of one negative interaction.**[38] If the ratio of positive to negative interactions starts to decline—for example, the negative interactions during the month outnumber the positive, a leader should examine the fit of this individual on the team.

3. Finally, **EVERY MONTH** leaders should learn each team member's top three goals for the month and should be updated on last month's three biggest accomplishments. While the onus of responsibility for steps one and two are on the leader, step three should be the obligation of the team member.

However, leaders should emphasize that it is not anticipated that the three-monthly goals will represent monumental achievements. Instead, these smaller goals will build upon one another and signify large annual accomplishments. Such a practice benefits both the leader and the team member. The leader is updated on the team member's accomplishments, and the team member can get credit for accomplishments that had, in the past, just been to-do lists on a calendar or in a notebook.

Accountability is Key

The Feedback Game Plan is built around the premise that a leader's number one job is to communicate about and hold team members accountable for their performance. It is not easy. The daily, weekly, and

---

[38] https://hbr.org/2013/03/the-ideal-praise-to-criticism

monthly schedule of feedback is time consuming, requires planning, and creates accountability—on the part of the leader and the team member. However, instilling this practice, and establishing such accountability, is exactly what improves each individual's performance and, ultimately, the organization as a whole.

Employees who strongly agree that their manager holds them accountable for their performance are 2.5 times more likely to be engaged.[39]

Leaders hold employees accountable. **Managers** do not. Instead, non-confrontational managers put off having difficult discussions with their employees or "forget" to mention an issue at a one-on-one meeting. However, a lack of accountability is a breeding ground for lower standards, decreased morale, and hard feelings toward team members who don't pull their weight.

Criticism or Critique?

Importantly, leaders do not confuse accountability with criticism. Instead, they use critiques to improve the performance of their team members and hold them accountable. While the difference between criticism and critique may seem small, it is quite profound. Former brigade combat team commander, Colonel (Ret) Mike Kasales is the rare street-smart and book-smart leader who appreciates the differences between these two similar-sounding terms.

Mike served for 28 years in the Army, completed multiple combat deployments in Afghanistan and Iraq, and relied heavily on critiques to build his team and improve himself. Mike believes criticism is more likely to be a managerial technique used by a civilian manager, and he

---

[39] Gallup, Inc. "3 Reasons Why Performance Development Wins in the Workplace." *Gallup.com*, www.gallup.com/workplace/231620/why-performance-development-wins-workplace.aspx.

believes it has no place in military leadership. Criticism is personal, biting, and tears people down: it serves as an attack. It's no wonder people become defensive when they are criticized. They feel the need to defend themselves in the face of this personal attack.

Critique is impersonal, outcome-specific, and geared to resolve less-than-perfect performance. Where criticism can be sarcastic, critique is objective and honest. Criticism comes from those who are looking for flaws to expose and weaknesses to shine a light on. Critique is delivered by those who are looking for clarification and want to find what's working and what's not.

Civilian leaders should take note of this distinction. While the stakes of business leadership may seem overwhelming at times, they pale in comparison to the responsibilities of a military leader who is ultimately responsible for the life of each team member. To protect these lives, the military leader's foremost objective is to create a team of highly skilled soldiers who deeply trust each other. Constant critique, not criticism, is the developmental tool used to achieve those objectives because, as this knowledgeable Colonel said, "No one gets ahead by putting someone down."

Summary

Chapter 3, the first chapter to introduce the FRESH leadership acronym, addresses the lifeblood that connects the leader and the team member: feedback. No one wants to be in the dark—wondering and worrying about their performance, how they are perceived, or what their boss really thinks of them. Frequent and honest critiques can help to eliminate this nonproductive speculation and move the leader-team member relationship in a trusting and positive direction. In chapter 4, we will address the need to couple positive feedback (when merited) with meaningful rewards.

Turning New Knowledge into Results

Below are questions that may help to improve the feedback that occurs between leaders and teams.

Leader Self-Examination Questions

1. Do you know the qualities that make each of your team members unique? Record at least three qualities that are special about each person. If this is a difficult or impossible task for you to complete, you need the help of an assessment.

2. How often do you give praise to your team members individually? Do you worry that too much praise will make them big-headed, arrogant, and lazy? Research shows the opposite is true. When managers provide daily feedback (versus annual feedback) their employees are three times more likely to be engaged at work.[40]

3. Create a list that categorizes the pros and cons of using The Feedback Game Plan. Do the pros outweigh the cons? What cons can you overcome? Could you convince another leader in your organization to partner with you and use The Feedback Game Plan for one month?

Group Discussion Questions

1. Positive feedback keeps us going in the right direction. Constructive feedback allows us to correct less than perfect

---

[40] Comaford, Christine. "Increase Employee Engagement By 300% With This Daily Practice." *Forbes*, Forbes Magazine, 5 May 2018, www.forbes.com/sites/christinecomaford/2018/04/14/leaders-increase-employee-engagement-by-300-with-this-daily-practice/.

performance. When have you received positive feedback that kept you motivated? When have you received constructive feedback that allowed you to improve?

2. Do you create daily or weekly "to-do" lists? What do you do with them when they are completed? Does anyone add completed tasks to the list that were not originally placed on the list? Why? Will anyone ever see your list? How might we use these lists to gain more insights into our team's daily and weekly accomplishments?

3. Being a good listener is an important quality. If we are able to listen to each other, to our customers, and to the world, we become more aware of our surroundings and the feelings of others. I'd like us to all think of one, two, or three things we could do to become better listeners.

Chapter Four
F.R.E.S.H. REWARDS

Brains, like hearts, go where they are appreciated.
–Robert McNamara, former Secretary of Defense

Everyone Wants the Right Birthday Cake

Do you remember, as a child, how important your birthday was? When I was little, I relished my birthday. I still have fond memories of playing pin-the-tail-on-the-donkey and drinking Hawaiian Punch (what a treat!) on that special day with friends and family at my birthday party. Like many children, and adults, I considered the grand finale of every birthday party to be blowing out the birthday candles on my special cake while making a wish.

My sisters and I had similar parties and engaged in similar activities with our guests over the years at our birthday celebrations, but one thing was always unique—our birthday cakes. My oldest sister—with her advanced taste buds—would frequently request rhubarb pie as her "cake." My middle sister always had yellow cake with chocolate frosting. I loved making the nontraditional request of pineapple upside-down cake and can still smell that baked pineapple and taste the gooey syrup, despite not having eaten the cake in a few decades.

I cannot even imagine how I would have felt if my mom had made me rhubarb pie for my birthday. Since I hated that odd-tasting pie, I imagine my emotions would have ranged from confusion to sadness to maybe even a bit of disgust. My mom, thank goodness, knew better than to give me my sister's special pie.

Knowing that someone will provide the right cake on your special day establishes a solid foundation of trust, love, and security. We appreciate when someone makes the effort to remember what is distinct about us (and our taste buds).

Leaders Are Pseudo-Parents at Work

The relevance of birthday cakes to leadership is this: leaders are pseudo- parents in the working world, and they need to be able to give the right cake to the right person on their team. Of course, I am not literally suggesting that leaders start baking cakes, but metaphorically, they should. Leaders need to think about each person on their team and find out what thrills, disappoints, delights, or dismays them.

Savvy leaders make an effort to understand the individual preferences and motivators that make each person distinct. As a leader, you want rewards to be like birthday cakes—unique to each person.

The challenge is determining what people want, but it's easier than you might think. The best way to find out what motivates team members is to ask them. It's possible they've never been asked that question before, and they'll appreciate dialogue about what rewards best suit them.

To get the discussion started, you may need to suggest different types of rewards. In appendix B, I provide a list of possible rewards organized into extrinsic and intrinsic categories. Use this list to help team members think about the types of rewards they prefer. However, before sharing the list with employees, take some time to customize it so the rewards match the options offered by your organization.

Giving the **right** reward shows a leader's appreciation, awareness, and familiarity with his or her team members. One size does **not** fit all when it comes to using rewards to motivate superior work. Most importantly, different types of rewards—both intrinsic and extrinsic rewards—should be used when selecting the best ways to motivate others.

Types of Rewards

As many book-smart leaders remember from learning about motivation, workers are motivated by both extrinsic and intrinsic rewards. Extrinsic rewards are rewards that come from outside of the employee. For example, money and nonmonetary benefits are common examples of extrinsic rewards.

Intrinsic rewards are internal or come from within the employee. (See appendix B for a list of Motivators at Work.) Pride in one's work and positive emotions felt after accomplishing a task are examples of intrinsic rewards. As many street-smart leaders know, and as was briefly discussed in chapter 1, employee motivations have shifted. People now want and expect work to be more than just a job: work needs to be meaningful. This is also an intrinsic reward.

Meaningful work is an intrinsic reward because it is related to personal pleasure as opposed to economic advancement. For instance, when a coaching client writes me a note of thanks, I am filled with pride and gratitude that I have been helpful. This note confirms that

I am making a meaningful difference and helping the individuals I coach, which makes me feel happy and accomplished.

Meaningful work is defined differently for each person. For some, meaning comes from learning new skills; for others, it comes from working with interesting or fun people; and for still others, it means making an impact on the lives of others. For tools that can help both leaders and team members better understand intrinsic motivation, go to appendices C and D where you'll find quizzes on Autonomy-Mastery-Purpose and Meaningful Work.

Traditional Rewards Theory

We have renowned behavioral psychologist B.F. Skinner to thank for giving us these insights into reward behavior and for coining the term. Skinner believed that "Behavior which is reinforced tends to be repeated; behavior which is not reinforced tends to die out or be extinguished."[41] Unlike other theories of motivation, Skinner's reinforcement theory does not take into account the inner feelings or drives of an individual. This theory's premise is that consequences, and consequences alone, influence behavior.

Skinner's theory of motivation, proposed in 1957, has had a direct impact on how many organizations advise leaders to manage their teams. **Leaders are told: reward the behaviors that support the goals of the organization and punish the behaviors that lead to unmet goals.** Recognition and praise, formal and informal awards, commission checks, bonuses, and promotional opportunities are ways that leaders put rewards to work.

---

[41] "B. F. Skinner." *Philip Zimbardo Facts & Biography | Famous Psychologists,* famouspsychologists.net/b-f-skinner/.

Two forms of punishment are regularly used by leaders: negative punishment and positive punishment. Both approaches attempt to reduce the observed behavior. For example, demotions and verbal reprimands are forms of positive punishment aimed at decreasing a behavior by giving an unfavorable response. Taking away privileges (like relaxed dress code or working from home) is a form of negative punishment aimed at decreasing a behavior by revoking incentives.

For today's leaders, rewarding behavior, instead of punishing behavior, is the preferred form of motivation for a number of reasons. **First, punishment, unlike rewards, does not help the leader improve work behavior.** Punishment merely attempts to extinguish poor or problematic behavior, without educating the employee about the correct behavior. An ineffective manager might say to a complaint-filled employee, "If you don't want your job, I'll find someone who does." Such a bullying phrase does nothing to help the worker address why they are complaining about work or improve the manager-employee relationship.

Second, punishment is frequently a short-term fix. Skinner found that problematic behavior frequently reappears after the punishment ends. For example, punishing an employee who frequently comes in late by asking them to clock-in for a period of time might improve their performance in the short-term—long enough to get back in her manager's good graces—but it would not be a long-term fix.

Motivation Theory

The importance of rewards—both tangible and intangible—cannot be overlooked at work. Pay is a good example of both a tangible and an intangible reward: we need money to support ourselves and our families but also because it represents status, freedom, or security.

Remarkably, studies have found that pay levels are not indicative of job satisfaction. In one study, reviewing 120 years of research, researchers found that people in the top half of the pay range had similar job satisfaction to people in the bottom half of the pay range.[42] **Ultimately, intrinsic motivation (new learning, the work itself) has been found to be a better predictor of job satisfaction than extrinsic motivation (cash bonus, award).**

Goals and Pay Can Do Harm

Daniel Pink's book on motivation, entitled *Drive: The Surprising Truth About What Motivates Us*, uncovers the many problems inherent in having goals connected to overly enticing extrinsic rewards.[43] It can lead to shortcuts and poor ethical decision-making. For example, sales quotas at Sears auto repair outlets encouraged staff to overcharge customers. The infamous executives at Enron profited from their unethical practices until those practices ended their business in 2001 and ultimately jailed 16 of these executives. These examples make us wonder, "What kind of person am I? Could I succumb to similar misdeeds?"

When people are internally rewarded by the activity itself (impressing customers, working on cutting-edge technology, helping people in need), it is less necessary to worry about shortcuts or lack of ethics. **Learning how to tap into the intrinsic rewards that motivate your individual team members is the most powerful way to unlock each person's full potential.**

---

[42] Chamorro-Premuzic, Tomas. "Does Money Really Affect Motivation? A Review of the Research." *Harvard Business Review*, 7 Aug. 2014, hbr.org/2013/04/does-money-really-affect-motiv.

[43] Pink, Daniel H. *DRIVE: The Surprising Truth about What Motivates Us.* Canongate books ltd, 2018.

Type X and Type I

Pink believes that there are two types of people. Type X individuals who are extrinsically motivated, and Type I people who are intrinsically motivated. The Type X folks are motivated by external things: money, fame, or status. They always want more and more. Old goals, once achieved, are just replaced by new, more difficult goals. In contrast, Type I's are driven internally: greater learning, a sense of accomplishment, pride in their work. Studies show that Type I's "have higher self-esteem, better interpersonal relationships, and greater physical and mental well-being." Appendix B contains a tool that allows for a subjective analysis of motivation.

Autonomy-Mastery-Purpose Trio: Pink also claims that when three important components are present in our work, we are more apt to be internally motivated and capable of doing our best work. These three elements are autonomy, mastery, and purpose but could also be defined as self-direction, a sense of improvement, and a focus on an outcome "bigger than ourselves." See appendix C for a tool to assess the presence or absence of each of these elements.

Meaningfulness of Work: The Work and Meaning Inventory[44] is a ten-item inventory created by Michael Steger which can help individuals quickly gauge the positive impact they believe their work has on themselves and the world.

Managers know that they need to be competitive when doling out external rewards (like pay increases, bonuses, and promotions). **Leaders are increasingly aware that having a competitive external rewards package is not enough to motivate today's workforce. They**

---

[44] "Measuring Meaningful Work: The Work and Meaning Inventory (WAMI)." *Journal of Research in Crime and Delinquency,* journals.sagepub.com/doi/abs/10.1177/1069072711436160.

need to couple superior external rewards with a good understanding of what intrinsic rewards motivate their team members, what type of team members they have on their team (Type X or Type I), and how meaningful the work is to each team member.

Values

Values play an enormous role in determining the meaningfulness of work. When individual values and work values are inconsistent or, worse yet, diametrically opposed, it is more likely that the individual will find work meaningless. Personal values and work values can clash when the individual has high standards related to professionalism or quality, and the organization encourages individuals to focus on short-term profits and frugality.

There are numerous examples of how a clash in values can play out in the workplace. Doctors and nurses who value the wellness and safety of their patients are forced to send at-risk patients home early. Lawyers who value helping clients are encouraged to focus on billable hours. Plumbers and electricians who value quality work are asked to work more efficiently and less thoroughly.

Learning about the values that drive each team member—emotional well-being, family, love, health, honesty, or knowledge—can allow leaders to tap into the rewards that connect with those values and examine the organizational messages that might minimize those values. Find out more about what values drive you by taking the VIA survey (www.ViaCharacter.org), a free online quiz that helps to identify the values that drive each individual.[45]

---

[45] "Latest News:" *Character Strengths, Character Building Experts: VIA Character,* www.viacharacter.org/www/.

Summary

In chapter 4, we considered the importance of rewarding each team member for their distinct service and abilities while simultaneously remembering the rewards that are most appreciated by them. Leaders are encouraged to investigate how their team members are motivated internally and externally as well as how their values impact the meaning they derive from work. In the next chapter, the median "E" in our FRESH acronym, Engagement, will be presented as a critical metric for FRESH leaders.

Turning New Knowledge into Results

The questions below are geared toward helping leaders and teams better understand the rewards that are most meaningful to them and why.

Leader Self-Examination Questions

In the past, what method(s) have you typically used to motivate your team members? After reading this chapter, what "new" motivational elements can you incorporate into your daily, weekly, or yearly motivational plans for your team?

To clarify what motivates you, take the following steps:
1. Determine if you are externally or internally motivated. Appendix B presents a list of extrinsic and intrinsic motivators. Which five motivators are most important to you?
2. Take the Autonomy-Mastery-Purpose Questionnaire in appendix C. Which items are most important to you? Why?

3. Meaningful work can have a variety of definitions. Take the Work and Meaning Inventory in appendix D not to determine how or why work is meaningful, but rather to consider the role work has in one's life. Do you consider your work meaningful? Do you consider the work of your team members to be meaningful? Why?

4. What are your top values? Do these values impact how or why you find your work meaningful? Go to appendix E to reflect on and define your core values.

Group Discussion Questions

1. Rewards are valued differently by different people. Sometimes it's hard to remember that we don't all value the same things. Take a look at the rewards listed in appendix B. Which five are most important to you?

2. Research shows that autonomy, mastery, and purpose help make work more internally motivating. Which of these three elements of work are most important to you? See appendix C for questions that may help you answer this question.

3. Finding meaning in our work is important. However, we may find different aspects of our work more meaningful than someone else. Our values play a role in the particular aspects of our job that we might find most rewarding or meaningful. Please use appendices D and E to evaluate how meaningful you find work and what values are most important to you. The VIA survey is also a good resource (www.ViaCharacter.org) to better understand your values. Does anyone want to share the connection between his or her values and the meaning derived from work?

Chapter Five

F.R.E.S.H. ENGAGEMENT

> *There are only three measurements that tell you nearly everything you need to know about your organization's overall performance: employee engagement, customer satisfaction, and cash flow.*
>
> **–Jack Welch, former CEO of General Electric**

Jack Welch was on to something here. Welch left the helm of General Electric in 2001, after 20 years of leading this organization and increasing its value by 4,000%. He understood the importance of checking the vitals of his organization. Notice how employee engagement is the first of the three critical factors he mentions in the quote above.

Employee Engagement Versus Employee Satisfaction

Employee engagement is a term that has multiple definitions. While the term "employee satisfaction" is similar, it is not as rich or as meaningful to the workplace or the employee as engagement. In the early 1990s, when I was fresh out of graduate school, assessing employee satisfaction was a cutting-edge practice. Organizations that considered themselves advanced in organizational behavior practices frequently performed **annual** employee satisfaction surveys to examine how employees felt about the organization from one year to the next.

Between 1990–2010, my business helped many organizations analyze their employees' satisfaction as well as develop strategies to improve future results. Leaders used the results of these assessments to better understand the organization's climate and to predict turnover, since employee satisfaction and employee retention have long been linked.

Gallup is the organization that coined the term "employee engagement" and brought this concept to the center stage of organizational development. **There is a critical distinction between employee engagement and employee satisfaction. Employee engagement has been found to promote increased productivity of employees while employee satisfaction merely explains how many employees are happy with their job and not looking to leave.**

Today, few organizations continue to measure only employee satisfaction. Leaders realize that, while a high retention rate is nice, having employees' who are both satisfied (and, therefore, not looking for another job) and engaged (and, therefore, productive) is the true goal.

What Does Engagement Look Like?

Gallup defines engaged employees as those who are involved in, enthusiastic about, and committed to their work and workplace.[46] While I appreciate this definition, I wonder how well it helps leaders

---

[46] Gallup, Inc. "Gallup Daily: U.S. Employee Engagement." *Gallup.com*, news.gallup.com/poll/180404/gallup-daily-employee-engagement.aspx

to visualize what an engaged workplace looks like. The problem is that most people understand that engaged employees are more likely to be enthusiastic about work but are unsure how that enthusiasm can be demonstrated on a daily basis by individual employees who may or may not be direct reports.

Can disengagement be detected merely by assessing an employee's lack of enthusiasm? Below are three scenarios that describe an employee's actions and why those actions are associated with engagement, lack of engagement, and disengagement.

Scenario 1: An employee drives to work and parks in the designated employee parking lot. As the employee walks toward the office building, she notices that there is an empty fast-food bag that has just missed the trash receptacle. The employee thinks, "Oh shoot, someone missed the trash bin. I'll put the bag in the trash as I walk into the building."

This employee is engaged at work. Unfortunately, only 33% of the workforce (according to Gallup) fits into this high-potential, high-energy, committed group.[47]

It makes no difference to the employee in this scenario that "trash pick-up" is not in her job description. She wants her workplace to look clean and professional. Picking up this discarded sack of fast food is not a normal part of her job, but she does not consider it to be a huge inconvenience or noteworthy in any way.

Scenario 2: An employee drives to work and parks in the designated employee parking lot. As the employee walks toward the office building, she notices that there is an empty fast-food bag that has just missed the trash receptacle. The employee thinks, "Oh shoot,

---

[47] Gallup, Inc. "Employee Experience vs. Engagement: What's the Difference?" *Gallup.com*, 12 Oct. 2018, www.gallup.com/workplace/243578/employee-experience-engagement-difference.aspx.

someone missed the trash bin. I'm sure the facility and maintenance people will be around soon to get it."

Trash pick-up is not in her job description, so she does not consider her inaction a lack of dedication. Her thought is "That trash is not my problem." **This employee is not engaged. Gallup's research shows that nearly half of all employees, 49%, are not engaged at work. Employees who are not engaged do the minimum required of them at work**. They see their job as a paycheck. They will put in their forty hours, but they will not do more than expected at work.

Scenario 3: An employee drives to work and parks in the designated employee parking lot. As the employee walks toward the office building, she notices that there is a trash receptacle where she can place her now empty fast-food bag. She attempts to make the "bucket," but her empty bag lands just a foot away from the bin. The employee thinks, "Oh shoot, I missed the trash bin. Just my luck. Is it Friday yet?"

This employee is actively disengaged. A sobering 18% of all workers are actively disengaged at work. Workers like the one described here are potential loose cannons at work because they can drag others down with them. **Actively disengaged employees are unhappy, and they demonstrate this unhappiness in their actions, words, and non-verbal communications, all-the-while bringing down the spirits of their colleagues.**

These three scenarios should inspire leaders to pay close attention to employee engagement. Some may question the financial impact of improving employee engagement. The return on investment is clear. **Research by McLean and Company found that while an engaged employee can return 120% on their salary in value, disengaged workers provide a mere 60% return on their salary in value.**[48]

---

[48] Stevens, Josh. "Engaging Employees, One Step at a Time." *Entrepreneur*, Entrepreneur, 16 Jan. 2015, www.entrepreneur.com/article/241865.

Employee engagement is a vital sign of organizational health. Below is a list of the many benefits of employee engagement, and the research that backs up these claims.

When groups in the top quartile of engagement were compared to groups in the bottom quartile of engagement, research has found:[49]

- **Increased safety** (engaged employees have 70% fewer incidents)
- **Better employee health** (engaged employees are less likely to be obese or have chronic health issues)
- **Lower absenteeism** (engaged employees have 41% lower absenteeism)
- **Higher retention rate** (engaged employees have 24% lower turnover)
- **Better quality** (engaged employees have 40% fewer quality defects)
- **Increased productivity** (engaged employees have 17% higher productivity)
- **Higher sales** (engaged employees have 20% higher sales)
- **Higher profitability** (engaged employees have 21% higher profitability)

Engagement Experts

Dreamworks, Southwest Airlines, Full Contact, Zappos, Facebook, Google, Quicken Loans, Intuit, Virgin, and REI are companies that are

---

[49] "2017 Gallup Employee Engagement Report: Surprising Results | TheEMPLOYEEapp." *Mobile Employee Communications and Engagement App*, 1 Nov. 2018, www.theemployeeapp.com/gallup-2017-employee-engagement-report-results-nothing-changed/.

setting the bar for all other organizations when it comes to researching, enacting new programs, and measuring employee engagement on a regular basis. Measuring engagement is as critical to these companies as measuring revenue.

These organizations realize that creating an engaged workforce does not happen overnight. An organization's efforts should start on day one of employment. Zappos, the shoe, clothing, and accessories company with 1,400 employees, aims for engagement from day one and is well-known for its positive workplace culture and high levels of employee engagement.

The company's well-regarded hiring and training program correlates to the ultimate engagement of its full-time employees. Zappos carefully selects new employees through a rigorous two-step interview process. If a candidate is then selected for a position, they immediately begin four weeks of paid training, during which they learn more about Zappos and their business philosophy. The training includes customer culture training, service training (for all positions), phone answering training (two weeks), and packing shoes into boxes training (one week).

At the end of the training period, new employees are asked to create a presentation that focuses on one or two of the company's values. This thorough training process results in a less than 1% dropout rate. The low dropout rate is even **more** surprising when one learns that at the very end of the four-week training, new hires are given the option to resign from the company with a $2,000 separation payment if they believe that they do not fit well with the Zappos culture. This is definitely a company focused on engaging employees from day one.

To Measure or to Not Measure

Organizations who measure engagement are attempting to get the pulse of the organization. Jack Welch's quote at the beginning of this chapter likens an engagement score to a vital sign of organizational health. We recognize that getting an annual medical examination to check blood work, review any changes in physical status, or get advice about possible problems is a best practice for good health. **Remarkably, employee engagement is a vital indicator of organizational health that can be overlooked or underestimated by some leaders.**

No Excuses

Zappos' efforts to engage its employees from their first day of employment may intimidate smaller businesses that have significantly fewer resources. I have spoken to many leaders over the years who are extremely hesitant to measure employee engagement for just this reason. They fear measuring employee engagement will shed light on an invisible—or at least an undefined—issue: lack of employee engagement.

Fearful of poor results, CEOs and team leaders skirt the issue. I have heard every excuse imaginable for not measuring employee engagement: "It's too expensive," "Our HR department is already stretched too thin," and even "If our employees learn that we have low engagement scores, morale will get even worse."

Instead of directly addressing just how engaged, not engaged, or disengaged staff is, the official process of measuring engagement is "put off" until there are more resources, morale seems better, or there is a fantastic year of profits. Enough stonewalling. Leaders must be brave enough to take the plunge and get a baseline number for employee engagement.

Diving into this world of measuring engagement means resisting the temptation to rely on gut instinct or leadership intuition to gauge the pulse of the organization. Operating in an employee engagement vacuum, with no data or statistical information about this critical piece of organizational health, is like assuming there is enough money in the bank account to make payroll this month without first checking the balance: it's irresponsible.

Many Tools to Choose From

Once you've committed to gauging employee engagement levels, the next step involves selecting an assessment tool. Over the past five years, a host of new engagement assessments have hit the marketplace. My preferred tool is the Gallup Q12, a 12-item employee engagement tool. While not new to the marketplace, the Q12 benefits from its access to Gallup's vast database of over 25-million employees from around the world. Using this tool allows your organization to tap into these benchmarking resources as well.

With that said, I encourage every organization to do their own due diligence and find the best tool for their unique environment: whether that means a need for weekly feedback, customized questions, or qualitative responses. Finding the right tool to measure engagement is your first step in the right direction.

Not a Silver Bullet

Forming a strategic initiative to measure engagement, finding the right assessment tool, and distributing it to employees on a regular basis is only the beginning. Unfortunately, just following these steps does not automatically guarantee that employee engagement scores will increase year after year. If only things were that easy … right?

Gallup started measuring engagement in US companies in 2000. Since that time, engagement of working people has been stable at about 33%.[50] However, there are organizations that have worked tirelessly to improve engagement and have an awe-inspiring 75% of employees who are engaged.

Of course, reaching these high levels of engagement is the exception and not the rule. Notably, Gallup has found that the **organizations who have dramatically increased their employees' engagement scores have two things in common: they follow up, and they choose managers wisely.**

Follow-Up Plans

Improving engagement levels requires more than simply administering surveys. Organizations need to follow up with a plan of action. This step can be challenging. Surveying employees is a time-consuming undertaking that requires planning, coordination among shifts and departments, and follow through to ensure as many employees as possible have the opportunity to participate.

Analyzing employee engagement results and explaining them to management and staff is the second, and too often final, wave of activity related to an employee engagement measurement program. It is not surprising that many organizations stop their efforts here, just short of crossing the real finish line.

However, to move an employee engagement program to the next level, companies need to keep going. The final and arguably most important step of employee engagement measurement should focus on the following two actionable items:

---

[50] Gallup, Inc. "U.S. Employee Engagement Slips Below 33% in May." *Gallup.com*, 10 June 2016, news.gallup.com/poll/192575/employee-engagement-slips-below-may.aspx.

1. Organizations need to create a training and development initiative that targets key areas for improvement identified by the survey results.
2. Organizations need to help leaders make practical changes in how they discuss the survey results and the initiative with their team.

For example, let's say that the engagement assessment finds that 44% of employees believe "that someone cares about my development at work," but the organization's goal is to have 75% of employees report that someone cares about their development.

A number of possible plans could be initiated to positively impact the employees' perceptions of how their skills are being developed. Possible initiatives include increasing the training budget for all departments, creating an internal cross-training program, or providing professional development counseling to all employees.

The critical **organizational** issue involves planning the specifics of this follow up. The critical **leadership** issue involves effectively and clearly communicating to team members that these new opportunities are available and that they are the direct result of the organization "hearing" the employees' needs and addressing them. Leaders make the opportunities more meaningful by connecting them to employees' needs.

Addressing engagement issues openly and non-defensively is challenging for some managers, who may take less-than-perfect results personally. Leaders, as opposed to managers, depersonalize the potentially ego-busting news that their team is not fully engaged by considering why some team members may have issues with the organization or with them.

For example, a leader may ask himself: "I wonder if Sam replied negatively to the development-related items on the engagement assessment since I had to deny his recent off-site training request." Another leader may think, "I know the team was disappointed by the quality of our last big project, this may have negatively impacted the engagement question that asked if we are committed to doing quality work."

In these situations, leaders strive to identify the different elements impacting their team's engagement and then work proactively to address these possible root causes. In the case of Sam, is it possible for him to obtain an off-site training this year or is there another way to develop Sam internally, such as a cross-training opportunity?

As for the team's perception of the organization's commitment to quality, it's important to discuss quality and the company's standards, the customer's needs, and the economic realities of specific projects. When employees are educated and informed about how quality-related business decisions are made, they are more likely to understand that less-than-optimal quality is an exception, not a rule.

Choose Leaders Wisely

The second common characteristic found in organizations with high employee engagement is the organization's ability to choose great leaders. Effective leaders create engaged teams, while ineffective managers create disengaged teams.

In fact, Gallup research (shown below) sheds tremendous light on why some teams thrive, but many flounder.

- **Managers account for 70% of the variance in employee engagement assessment.**[51]
- **The right candidates for leadership positions are selected only 18% of the time.**

---

[51] Gallup, Inc. "Managers Account for 70% of Variance in Employee Engagement." *Gallup.com*, 21 Apr. 2015, news.gallup.com/businessjournal/182792/managers-account-variance-employee-engagement.aspx.

Managers have an enormous impact on employee engagement, which makes choosing the right people for positions of leadership so critical. Leaders, unlike managers, want to develop people and see the role of leadership as an opportunity, not a burden.

The old rules state that those with seniority and specialized expertise—people who've been around a long time and may have industry-specific knowledge—should oversee the newer and/or less-seasoned employees. However, individuals with expertise and experience should not become leaders by default. While these qualities are critical pieces of an organization, they do not necessarily qualify someone to be an effective leader.

Today's leaders should be talented individuals who are passionate about growing the business and developing people. A frequent complaint I hear from an overwhelmed manager is, "I have so much work to do that I cannot possibly give my team frequent feedback." This complaint reveals an underlying reason for many managers' ineffectiveness: they have not yet created a team capable of accomplishing the "to-do" list of duties, which would free up the manager to be a supportive developer of the team.

Informal leaders, those individuals who do not have direct reporting responsibilities but seem to be go-to question-answerers, are frequently the candidates who are best equipped for a formal role in leadership. These informal leaders intuitively understand how to empower others to get their work done, get satisfaction from helping others, and understand boundaries: they don't take on too much work for themselves.

Impactful Leadership

Let's see how these statistics about leadership can impact a company. Dave, a newly promoted manager for a regional bank, was an up-and-coming private banker in the early 2000s who initially served as an informal leader to his peers. When his superiors noticed Dave's great potential, he was included in the bank's leadership training program.

Soon thereafter, Dave was given a choice—remain in his current city and be among a handful of candidates who would vie for his boss's job in a few years or receive a promotion immediately, move to the northern part of the state, and oversee 32 people and three branches.

Dave was leaning toward the promotion-now option, despite his peers' warnings that this position in the north was a "death sentence" for his career. His peers knew that the northern region banks were known for two things: terrible engagement scores and terrible financial results. In fact, the northern banks were 24th overall in revenue growth, which meant they were last. They ranked 24th out of 24 banking regions.

Dave accepted the promotion with his eyes wide open. He was fully aware of the challenges before him and recognized that he had no prior experience addressing either of the pressing issues that needed to be rectified. However, Dave had knowledge. He was not operating in a vacuum. Annual engagement scores and frequent updates on the bank's revenue growth were at his fingertips. He just needed to concoct a plan to improve these scores.

Dave's predecessor, let's call her Negative Nelly, was a lifer at the bank, promoted under the old-school rules of seniority. She was well connected to many of the prominent business owners in the small towns that these three banks served and used her social prowess like a machete—to cut down others in her path.

Negative Nelly welcomed Dave on his first day with these frigid words, "This region hates new faces, and they will hate you." It soon became clear to Dave that this icy welcome was indicative of how she had treated the 32 employees she had overseen for the last year.

By treating others with indifference and disdain, Negative Nelly showed that she did not think work needed to be meaningful or fun. She did not consider staff development a privilege of her position, and she was quick to point out deficiencies and slow to notice good work. Dave's improvement plan was, thus, informally created: to be the anti-Negative Nelly.

Over the course of the next year, Dave replaced his region's culture of blame and negativity with understanding and fun. He brought in Gallup trainers to help him and all 32 employees better understand team dysfunction and disengagement. He created a fun committee that organized Wii boxing and office triathlons. More importantly, he took the advice of his smart administrative assistant, Nancy, and started meeting with his employees on an individual basis every week.

Dave took to heart Nancy's advice that Dave could seem "intense" in a group setting. Nancy recognized that Dave's helpfulness and caring—Dave's real personality—could best shine in one-on-one meetings. Initially, Dave had believed he could win over small groups (for example, the bank tellers) and then move on to the next work group.

Nancy was insightful enough to recognize that this method was not making the impact Dave needed. Dave hated small talk but loved learning about the specific needs of each team member and creating a plan to meet their needs. Nancy scheduled weekly one-hour meetings with each team member to play to Dave's strengths (creating one-on-one connections, learning about people), and to eliminate, or at least diminish, the dreaded small talk meetings in the bank's hallways.

Bottom line: after three years of work, Dave's region saw significant increases in both engagement (taking engagement from a grand mean of 2.89 to 4.0) and revenue growth (taking revenue growth from being 24th out of 24 to being among the top 10). Dave was successful in transforming this region's work culture and financial performance in just three short years.

Dave proved that he was much more than an inexperienced manager. He was a real leader. His leadership was manifested when he chose to use insightful (but to some leaders potentially threatening) feedback from a direct report to play to his strengths as a manager and better understand the needs and strengths of each employee.

Summary

Chapter 5, Engagement, delves into the nuts and bolts of how to foster inspiration and enthusiasm at work. The example of a new manager, Dave, transforming an underperforming and disengaged team into a high-performing and engaged team, shows the remarkable potential that awaits eager leaders who are determined to make a difference. Dave's intuitive understanding of leadership—that his role as a leader required him to serve his employees and their needs—will be discussed in greater depth in Chapter 6.

Turning New Knowledge into Results

The questions below are posed to help leaders and teams think more specifically about what engagement looks and feels like-within their organization and outside of it.

Leader Self-Examination Questions

1. Does your organization measure employee engagement? Why or why not? What are the "reasons" used to explain why engagement is overlooked? Expense? Logistics? Value?

2. How might low engagement (measured or unmeasured) be costing your organization in salaries, safety, employee health, and profits?

3. Does your organization have its own version of Negative Nelly in a managerial role? How might this individual be negatively impacting your organization's overall engagement?

Group Discussion Questions

1. We have all heard about organizations that make big efforts to engage their employees. Dreamworks, Southwest Airlines, Full Contact, Zappos, Facebook, Google, Quicken Loans, Intuit, Virgin, and REI are among some of the leading organizations when it comes to engagement. Let's talk about our personal experiences as customers of these organizations. What can we learn from them? Are there ways for our team to emulate some of their good practices?

2. There are examples on pages 74-77 of what an engaged, not engaged, and actively disengaged employee looks like at work. If our organization is like most, only one-third of our employees are engaged. Do you think it's possible to create a culture where engagement is the norm and not the exception? What changes would you suggest?

Chapter Six
F.R.E.S.H. SERVICE

*Growth and development of people is
the highest calling of leadership.*

–Harvey S. Firestone, founder of the Firestone Tire and Rubber Company

The Servant-Leader Paradox

In the world of organizational behavior, the term servant-leader has been overused to the point of being passé. Despite this fact, I cannot keep myself from discussing this term as an essential piece of what distinguishes a leader from a manager.

Surprisingly, the terms "servant-leader" and "servant leadership" continue to be misunderstood and dismissed as irrelevant by many who may not have a full understanding of the concept. Managers may be aware of the term but **mistakenly** assume that a servant-leader just caters to the whims of his or her team. Nothing could be further from the case.

As book-smart leaders may know, the concept of servant-leadership originated in 1970 with Robert E. Greenleaf's essay "The Servant as Leader."[52] Lesser known facts about servant-leadership and its author include that Bob was a nice man from Terre Haute, Indiana, and that his tombstone reads, "Potentially a good plumber, ruined by a sophisticated education." Bob wrote these words—his epitaph. It's hard not to like someone who is funny, even at the end.

But, more importantly, Greenleaf's once revolutionary ideas regarding leadership continue to be relevant 50-plus years after "The Servant as Leader" was published. There are ten characteristics of servant-leadership that a book-smart leader may have once known and has now forgotten.

Although all ten characteristics are important (and I've listed all ten and a mini-definition below), three stand out as thoroughly relevant to leaders and their need to serve the people they lead. These three characteristics of note are in bold.

Characteristics of Servant-Leadership

1. Listening – Listen intently to others.
2. Empathy – Strive to empathize with others.
3. Healing – Heal emotional hurts.
4. Awareness – Self-awareness and awareness of others (especially as this connects to ethics and values).
5. Persuasion – Instead of relying on authority, convince others. Avoid coercion at all costs.

---

[52] "What Is Servant Leadership?" *Greenleaf Center for Servant Leadership*, www.greenleaf.org/what-is-servant-leadership/.

6. Conceptualization – Dream great dreams. Share these dreams.
7. Foresight – Using lessons of the past, understand and foresee the likely outcome in the future.
8. Stewardship – Serve the needs of others, first and foremost.
9. Commitment to the growth of people – Make time and resources available to encourage personal and professional development in others.
10. Building community – Create a workplace community that can fill the void that has opened up from a lack of local community.

While it is difficult to sideline seven of these ten characteristics, rest assured that a few of the above characteristics (listening, awareness, and persuasion) have already been touched upon in previously discussed areas of the FRESH acronym. Two others—empathy and building community—will be highlighted in the next chapter on human connection.

Service—Why Now?

Leaders, unlike managers, recognize that service to and for employees directly impacts their ability to retain talent. It's similar to how superior customer service results in the retention of prime customers. As discussed in chapter 2, expectations have changed. Employees have higher expectations for their job and expect fulfillment in that role.

Today, if a team member receives a review from a manager who is uninspiring and lacks awareness of his or her goals (both personal and professional), the team member may start searching for a new job and a more compelling and encouraging leader.

Three major changes in employment have resulted in a tipping of the scales in favor of the employee and away from the employer. These changes include:[53]

1. Historic lows in unemployment (the second lowest point in 40 years) make jobs readily available.
2. Workplace transparency made possible by online organizational reviews posted on Glassdoor, LinkedIn and Facebook increases employees' abilities to evaluate and compare workplace cultures.
3. Job search engines (like Indeed, Monster, Simply Hired, and CareerBuilder) coupled with online job applications make the once challenging job search process relatively simple for computer literate applicants.

These changes illuminate why service to employees is needed today more than ever before. Additionally, much like the need for leaders to personalize feedback (discussed in chapter 3) and rewards (presented in chapter 4), leaders must also personalize the best way to serve each team member. **Service from a leader to an employee can be achieved by delighting, developing, and respecting them on an individual and group basis.**

Delight

Why would a leader want to delight her team, and what can she do to achieve such a lofty goal? When such questions are posed about

---

[53] Finkelstein, Jason. "2018: Companies Who Don't Treat Employees like Customers Will Eventually Fail." *HR Technologist*, www.hrtechnologist.com/articles/employee-engagement/2018-companies-who-dont-treat-employees-like-customers-will-eventually-fail/.

the need to delight customers, the answers seem obvious. A delighted customer is a happy customer. Customer delight occurs when the customer is surprised by the level of care shown by the organization.

When a customer's expectations are exceeded, the emotion of delight can be triggered. This emotional reaction can, in turn, have positive outcomes, including:

- Increased customer loyalty
- Create a more profitable experience
- Promote customers to publicly endorse the organization or product

Leaders who inspire employee delight can benefit from the same far-reaching and positive responses. When employees are delighted by their leaders, they are surprised by the level of care that their leader has shown. This surprise triggers an emotional response that can mirror the delighted customer's reactions by increasing loyalty to the leader, creating more profitable experiences, and motivating the employee to publicly praise the leader inside and outside the organization.

The willingness to "go the extra mile" to delight a team is what separates a leader from a manager. One friend, a leader who owns multiple breakfast restaurants, literally and figuratively served his team of cooks, waiters, dishwashers, and hostesses. He treated them to a sit-down, no-work, Italian dinner personally prepared by this leader and his restaurant managers.

Another leader, a doctor with a large office staff, delighted his team of nurses, receptionists, and billing specialists by buying and personally delivering lunch to them every Friday. As a way to sweeten an already good deal, the doctor let them leave early with the time gained by not going off-site during the lunch hour.

Food, of course, is not the only way to delight staff, it's just the easiest. Below are a few great ideas that can build individual goodwill and team community while simultaneously delighting team members:

1. Off-site team building
    a. Ropes course/zipline
    b. Escape room experience
    c. Painting or pottery making as a group
    d. All-day volunteering opportunities (e.g., Habitat for Humanity)
2. Celebrate milestones (large and small)
    a. Babies
    b. Accomplishments (marathons, civic involvement)
    c. Certifications and degrees
    d. Anniversaries
    e. Birthdays
3. Notes of thanks
    a. Handwritten
    b. Email
    c. Text
    d. Social media
4. Learn something new
    a. Go to a conference as a team
    b. Tour a high-caliber organization (Google's Googleplex headquarters, Zappos Tour Experience, HERSHEY'S Chocolate Tour)

c. Ask each team member to put on a 15-minute crash-course seminar of their choice. Topics could be industry-related tips (for example, the best new online tools) or fun and experiential activities (for example, to judge the best donut holes in town based on four samples).

Delighting staff is indicative of a leader who fundamentally wants to have fun with and show appreciation for her team members.

Develop

Leaders not only recognize the need to develop team members, they also search for ways to provide this development. Managers, who are less focused on the importance of development, expect team members to engage in self-development and may only provide appropriate training to those who request it. The distinction here between a leader and a manager is which one takes ownership and responsibility for development. A leader accepts this responsibility. A manager relinquishes this responsibility.

To actively develop others takes vision, planning, and a commitment to others, as noted in the ten characteristics of servant leadership. A leader must consider not only where the business will be in the future, but also how each team member's capabilities can be developed to meet these future demands. This involves creating long-term and short-term development plans.

When leaders strategically develop their teams' knowledge base and capabilities, everyone wins—the leader, the team, and the organization. Conversely, when staff development is treated as an add-on or ignored, employees and the company lose.

Studies by Towers Watson over a five-year period show that if high-performing individuals are given career development opportunities and are aware of long-term career opportunities, their profitability and opinion scores soar.[54] However, research shows that most employees do not have a leader who recognizes and champions their progress and growth at work.

On average, only three in 10 employees strongly agree that there is someone at work who encourages their development.[55]

Leaders need to approach team members with a "What can I do for you today?" attitude rather than a "What have you done for me lately?" approach. Those who misunderstand the servant-leadership model might see this shift in attitude as signaling an inability to lead, a weakness, or a lack of control over a team. On the contrary, it is a sign of power. Leaders should have the confidence and feel secure enough with their authority to make insightful suggestions or real-time changes that can directly impact team members' effectiveness.

Development, from this vantage point, is both a short-term and long-term endeavor. Leaders want to help their team members achieve success today and in the future, which means looking at day-to-day operations as well as planning for future skills. One talented leader may help a team member by connecting her with the right people—internally and externally—to facilitate her success on a challenging project. Another savvy leader may plan for the future and consider how to best harness the strengths of a gifted team member to enhance his career in the long-term.

---

[54] "U.S. Employees Give Senior Leadership Low Marks, Willis Towers Watson Research Reveals." *Willis Towers Watson*, www.willistowerswatson.com/en/press/2017/06/us-employees-give-senior-leadership-low-marks.

[55] Gallup, Inc. "Give Performance Reviews That Actually Inspire Employees." *Gallup.com*, 25 Sept. 2017, www.gallup.com/workplace/236135/give-performance-reviews-actually-inspire-employees.aspx.

Respect

Another way leaders can serve their teams is by showing respect for each and every team member. Respect and leadership are intertwined. To become a true leader, one must demonstrate respect—for oneself and others. Unfortunately, research shows that some powerful people in the workplace who have the title "leader" do not meet this basic requirement of leadership. **A *Harvard Business Review* study found that 54% of 20,000 employees worldwide <u>do not</u> "regularly get respect from their leaders."**[56]

Not surprisingly, respect and engagement are highly correlated. In fact, the same study found that **respect is the most important leader behavior to impact employee engagement**—more important than employee recognition, communicating a vision, giving feedback, or making opportunities for growth.

Respect is connected to emotions because one either **feels respect or does not feel respect**. The leadership behaviors that signify respect may be different for various individuals and are impacted by age, gender, and culture. A leader must consider how to best communicate respectful feelings based on the specific needs of each team member.

Being respectful takes effort. An important distinction to note is that the absence of disrespect does not necessarily mean that team members feel respected. Leaders need to show and practice respectful behavior. It engages team members and creates an environment where respecting others is the accepted norm.

---

[56] Porath, Christine. "Half of Employees Don't Feel Respected by Their Bosses." *Harvard Business Review*, 6 Dec. 2017, hbr.org/2014/11/half-of-employees-dont-feel-respected-by-their-bosses

Below are a number of ways that leaders can intentionally show respect to team members.

Respectful Leadership Behaviors

1. Listen with thoughtfulness and attention to the needs of the speaker.
2. Say thank you. Show appreciation.
3. Never squash ideas.
4. Do not create an in group (favorite team members) and an out group (less than favorite team members). The out group will feel disrespected.
5. Praise, praise, praise—publicly and privately.

Finding Your Why and Their Why

The street-smart leader understands that one of the most fulfilling parts of leadership is helping others. Martin Luther King, Jr., said, "Life's most persistent and urgent question is, 'What are you doing for others?'" He realized that leadership was not about self-aggrandizement, power, or control. It was about helping others to succeed. King is also a leader who inspired others by asking them to start with why.

Simon Sinek's book, *Start with Why: How Great Leaders Inspire Everyone to Take Action*, gained attention from many business book readers who recognized the importance of his message.[57] He encouraged people to consider why we do the things we do. From this understanding, we gain purpose both at work and at home, and fulfillment enters into our lives.

---

[57] Sinek, Simon. *Start with Why: How Great Leaders Inspire Everyone to Take Action.* Portfolio/Penguin, 2013.

Similarly, when leaders help team members understand why an organization does what it does, why it exists, why customers keep coming back, and why they are an important piece of that complex puzzle, they begin to understand how work is more than something they **have** to do. It becomes something they **want** to do. Work becomes inspiring and meaningful.

Ask Why

To help others find meaning in their work, an easy way to start the conversation is to repetitively ask "why." For example, ask your organization's receptionist "Why do you answer the phones?" and continue to follow up with probing "why" questions until you hit upon the meaningful nugget that makes the job purposeful.

Chip and Dan Heath, authors of *The Power of Moments: Why Certain Experiences Have Extraordinary Impact*, explain that this technique can help expose the purpose of a job that may not be as obvious as, say, the purpose of a heart surgeon's job.[58]

Below, the Heath brothers show how this technique can be used to help a hospital janitor find meaning in his or her position. Please note, it is imperative that the question-based interaction be both positive and congenial. If not, the question-asker risks taking on the role of inquisitor, instead of the role of helpful leader:

Why do you clean hospital rooms? "Because that's what my boss tells me to do." Why? "Because it keeps the rooms from getting dirty." Why does that matter? "Because it makes the rooms more sanitary and more pleasant." Why does that matter? "Because it keeps the patients healthy and happy."

---

[58] Heath, Dan. *The Power of Moments*. Random House UK, 2017.

Summary

In chapter 6, the importance of service—the service of the leader to the employee and the service of the employee to the world—is examined. Leaders understand that facilitating the growth of their team members and unlocking the meaning behind the work they do daily is more than a nice to have.

These are need-to-have components in order to have a purposeful workplace and an engaged team. Below are questions to help leaders and team members gain more insight into how serving others is connected to meaningful work. In chapter 7, Human Connection, the old-school rule that "all emotions at work should be masked" is questioned.

Turning New Knowledge into Results

The leader and discussion questions below touch on ways to find meaning at work.

Leader Self-Examination Questions

1. Have you ever had a manager who put his or her needs first and the team members' needs last? How would you describe that experience?

2. Who in your life has been the most encouraging and supportive of your growth and development as a person? As a professional? What is most memorable about that person??

3. What is your why? How might you help others discover their why?

Group Discussion Questions

1. There is a great Forbes article about finding your why. In it, the author, Margie Warrell, asks her reader to consider four questions.[59] Let's do the same:

   - What makes you come alive?
   - What are your inner strengths? (If this is difficult for you to answer, consider taking the Clifton Strengths assessment: www.GallupStrengthsCenter.com.)
   - Where do you add the greatest value?
   - How will you measure your life?

2. How can we use the answers above to find more meaning at work and connect our "why" with our professional lives?

---

[59] Warrell, Margie. "Do You Know Your 'Why?' 4 Questions To Find Your Purpose." *Forbes*, Forbes Magazine, 17 Apr. 2014, www.forbes.com/sites/margiewarrell/2013/10/30/know-your-why-4-questions-to-tap-the-power-of-purpose/

Chapter Seven

F.R.E.S.H. HUMAN CONNECTION

The hardest thing about being a leader is demonstrating or showing vulnerability ... When the leader demonstrates vulnerability and sensibility and brings people together, the team wins.

–Howard Schultz, CEO of Starbucks

The Difference Between Being Frail and Being Vulnerable

No one wants to appear frail or unsteady. Leaders are certainly not immune from this desire. However, we connect most effectively on a human level with our friends, neighbors, spouses, and workmates when we can be authentic. Authenticity means seeing the good and the bad, the strengths and the weaknesses, the highs and the lows in a person's life.

Leaders are often unaccustomed to sharing the negative aspects of their lives: the bad, the weaknesses, and the lows. Old work rules claim that leaders are strong and invincible, but today's employees want and need to connect to their leader on a human level. They need a leader who is vulnerable.

In recent years, notable business leaders have challenged the "leader-is-invincible" posture by taking chances and sharing their vulnerabilities with their teams and the public. As a result, they became better connected with those around them. Howard Schultz and Sheryl Sandberg are two well-known and revered leaders who have both shown vulnerability when they encountered a crisis and emerged better leaders for their trials and tribulations, honesty, and openness. Schultz was part of Starbucks' historic business decline, while Sandberg dealt with the unexpected death of her spouse. Sandberg has acknowledged that while most leaders do not seek out ways to show their vulnerability, she feels that since her husband's death she is "much closer to the people around (her) than (she) was."[60]

A mediocre manager hides weaknesses and pretends to be covered in Teflon. Nothing can penetrate the façade that everything is perfect (at work and at home), and his demeanor is unflappable. A strong leader shows his humanity and imperfections in a way that is not pitiful or painful, but in a way that connects with the surrounding people.

Separate crises forced the hands of Schultz and Sandberg and encouraged (or possibly required) them to show their vulnerability. However, any leader can become authentically and effectively vulnerable—while remaining professional and appropriate.

---

[60] McGregor, Jena. "The Leadership Lessons in Sheryl Sandberg's and Adam Grant's New Book about Resilience and Grief." *The Washington Post*, WP Company, 25 Apr. 2017, www.washingtonpost.com/news/on-leadership/wp/2017/04/25/the-leadership-lessons-in-sheryl-sandbergs-and-adam-grants-new-book-about-resiliency-and-grief/.

Below are a few practical examples of how to show vulnerability in the workplace.

1. **Apologize**—When leaders apologize, they are admitting their shortcomings (and demonstrating confidence). When managers refuse to apologize, they are ignoring their transgression (and demonstrating insecurity). Apologize for being late to a one-on-one meeting. Apologize for not responding to a request immediately.

2. **Model desirable work-balance behaviors**—Leaders need to model the behaviors they claim to want their team members to adhere to in the workplace—staying home when sick, not checking email on vacation, prioritizing a non-work activity, etc.

3. **Discuss failures**—Learning about a leader's important failures on her way to greatness is reassuring. All great leaders know that failure can be an instrumental tool—a teachable moment—on one's way to the top. Survival, endurance, renewal, and learning are all takeaways that can be gleaned from any "epic failure."

4. **Ask for help**—When a manager doesn't know what to do next, they do nothing. When a leader doesn't know what to do next, they ask for help.

It can take years of practice to get good at asking for help. Great leaders know where they need help most and are not afraid to look to their team members to help them navigate the mine fields that are most problematic for them. In Chapter 8, the topic of how to compensate for blind spots will be discussed at length.

Vulcans at Work No More

Do you remember Spock from the television series (and later movies) *Star Trek*? Spock was a fictional Vulcan being who had no emotions. Spock was never going to get misty-eyed from sadness, need to blow off steam from anger, or have that look of love in his eye. It drove viewers, like me, insane.

The character Spock was integral to the cast of *Star Trek* because he could make decisions using only logic and reason. The rest of the human characters on the spaceship were not immune from their emotions, and Spock was the point person for getting an unemotional read on what to do in a critical situation.

When I first entered the workforce in 1991, the Vulcan-vibe prevailed. Emotions were not discussed or willingly demonstrated at work. Most people, myself included, seemed to have a professional mask that they wore at work. This mask was thought to help people to be productive. Formality and emotional detachment prevailed.

Some psychologists, in particular Stephanie Mitrano in her fascinating TedTalk entitled "Emotions at Work", suggest that this lack of empathy and need for emotional control at work encourages psychopathic behavior.[61] While some might think that is an extreme conclusion, it is at least a partial explanation for why masking our emotions at work is so uncomfortable.

A new consensus of workplace psychologists and organizational behavior specialists has found that emotions in the workplace can be powerful when used productively. For example, anger, if controlled and channeled, can spur dramatic change. Martin Luther King, Jr., did just

---

[61] Talks, TEDx. "Emotions at Work | Stéphanie Mitrano | TEDxToulon." *YouTube*, YouTube, 12 Sept. 2014, www.youtube.com/watch?v=xtDf6YIS_gM.

that. Storytelling, when used to connect to a customer or invigorate a team, is also best received when it taps into emotions and connects the audience to the storyteller.

Leaders need to be real at work. Every leader can start the practice of being more approachable and human immediately. Instead of responding to a question about the weekend with a bland and emotionless, "It was good. Great weather," a leader who is trying to establish an authentic connection will talk about something that happened and how she felt about it. For example, "It was good. I'm teaching my son to ride a bike. It was frustrating and exhausting. He has skinned knees, but we got it done. The whole process really made me think about my dad a lot." Inserting human candor, where before there was masked, polite, and businesslike chit-chat, can create a foundation for future discussions about more substantive issues, like values, goals, and the meaning of work. More importantly, this first step can happen the next time you go to work.

Emotional Intelligence is a Leadership Imperative

As book-smart and street-smart leaders know, emotional intelligence is the new catchphrase that business people use in their conversations to mean "people-smart." Emotional intelligence is defined in textbooks as one's ability to understand one's emotions and the emotions of someone else. Despite book-smart and street-smart leaders' awareness of the need for emotional intelligence—and its cousin empathy—at work, both skills are greatly underutilized in the workplace.

Daniel Goleman, the father of emotional intelligence, and his colleague Richard Boyayzkis have **found that "there is a large performance gap between the socially intelligent and socially**

unintelligent leaders."[62] Ignoring emotions at work does not make emotions disappear. In fact, the opposite is true. Stress at work occurs when emotions are suppressed because workers do not have support from their manager or colleagues.[63] The world needs leaders who are willing to address the emotions of their team and support their concerns.

Create an Emotionally Intelligent Team

Unfortunately, the need to address emotions at work is often minimized by managers who do not think emotions have a place at work. Recently, while I was working with a manager and her team, the manager questioned how empathy could be used productively and professionally in her straight-laced, male-dominated, and unemotional banking environment. I explained how being aware of the emotions in a room (like fear, confusion, sadness, stress, and the like) can help start a conversation that ultimately promotes individual and team productivity.

As a leader, it can be tough to honestly address the emotions and feelings in a room and then start a conversation about them. We've all been in meetings where ignored discord has prevented progress. One way a leader can address these emotions is by saying, "I'm noticing some negative body language in the room; possibly there is not as much agreement about this issue as we have verbalized. Can anyone give me their thoughts on this?" Leaders capable of identifying emotional

---

[62] Asghar, Rob. "How Good Managers Manage Emotions." *Forbes*, Forbes Magazine, 9 June 2014, www.forbes.com/sites/robasghar/2014/04/25/how-good-managers-manage-emotions/.

[63] "Stress at the Workplace." *World Health Organization*, World Health Organization, 8 Dec. 2010, www.who.int/occupational_health/topics/stressatwp/en/.

discomfort and asking for feedback are light-years ahead of those who brush off or ignore the silent messages that are often more important than the overt discussions.

Compensate for Deficiencies

Leaders who are aware of their inability to read the emotions of others need to manage around this issue. We'll discuss how to do this in greater depth in chapter 8. Until then, know that leaders who understand their weaknesses have a unique opportunity. The leader is in a position to find a partner, or partners, capable of providing candid insights that the leader might miss if left to her own devices.

A great example of how to make this suggestion actionable comes from a leader, Tim, who told his team members to always begin a conversation with him by explaining how they felt about the situation. Tim recognized that he frequently misunderstood or didn't recognize the emotions of others. However, his brilliant solution was to address this deficiency in a straightforward and direct way.

By making this request of his team, Tim capably hit three birds with one stone. First, he openly addressed the importance of each team members' emotions. His request showed that he wanted to know what their emotions were, but like someone who cannot hear a certain pitch, he could not understand or intuit their emotions without being told.

Second, he acknowledged his deficiency. As discussed previously in this chapter, pretending to be a perfect and completely self-sufficient leader can harm the team. Discussing any deficiency shows a healthy vulnerability that increases trust, acceptance, and human connection between the leader and the team members.

Third, he modeled behavior that is critical to effective teamwork but is difficult for many leaders to do—he asked for help. Frequently, strong-willed and successful leaders associate asking for help with weakness. Of course, asking for help is actually a sign a mental toughness and strength.

As was discussed in chapter 2, it's important for today's leaders to create a fair and trusting environment while promoting mutual respect (especially when it comes to communication). Team members who trust one another are less likely to be defensive and are better able to consider someone else's emotions. Ultimately, when team members are accustomed to having their opinions listened to, they are more apt to respect the team's commitment to listening to everyone else's ideas.

Loneliness at Work Is an Epidemic

The famous psychologist Carl Jung is well known for saying, "Loneliness does not come from having no people around you, but from being unable to communicate the things that seem important to you."[64] Jung recognized that proximity to other human beings did not predict a lack of loneliness or, in contrast, an abundance of loneliness.

Common sense might predict that social connections are better than ever at work, particularly given the increased emphasis on teamwork in the last 20+ years. Sadly, social connections that are seemingly accessible at work are on the decline. *Forbes* magazine, in a 2017 article entitled "3 Reasons Employee Engagement is Declining – and How Managers Can Improve It," claims that only "24% of employees 'feel strongly connected to their co-workers,' an 11% drop from the prior year."[65]

---

[64] Jung, C. G., and Jaffé Aniela. *Memories, Dreams, Reflections*. Fontana Paperbacks, 1983.

[65] Lipman, Victor. "3 Reasons Employee Engagement Is Declining -- And How Managers Can Improve It." *Forbes*, Forbes Magazine, 1 Feb. 2017, www.forbes.com/sites/victorlipman/2017/02/01/3-reasons-employee-engagement-is-declining-and-how-managers-can-improve-it/.

A *Harvard Business Review* article suggests that burnout and workplace loneliness are connected. More than twice as many people say they are "always exhausted" today, as compared to 20 years ago.[66] The article by Emma Seppala and Marissa King states that, "There is a significant correlation between feeling lonely and work exhaustion: The more people are exhausted, the lonelier they feel."

A related study by the health insurer Cigna concurs with this idea and claims that loneliness is rampant in America with **nearly 50% of respondents claiming that they feel alone or left out always or sometimes.**[67] **Possibly more important is the shocking finding from this same study that "loneliness has the same impact on mortality as smoking 15 cigarettes a day, making it even more dangerous than obesity."**

Camaraderie

How can leaders address this loneliness epidemic? How can leaders create interdependence among team members and an environment that breeds more than mere congeniality? How can leaders help create connections and authentic friendships? Finding commonalities between people who may appear on the surface to be polar opposites involves embracing the differences among team members and finding humor in human error. These behaviors are just a few of the ways that leaders can foster such an environment.

---

[66] King, Emma SeppäläMarissa, et al. "Burnout at Work Isn't Just About Exhaustion. It's Also About Loneliness." *Harvard Business Review*, 27 Nov. 2017, hbr.org/2017/06/burnout-at-work-isnt-just-about-exhaustion-its-also-about-loneliness.

[67] Tate, Nick. "Loneliness Rivals Obesity, Smoking as Health Risk." WebMD, *WebMD*, 4 May 2018, www.webmd.com/balance/news/20180504/loneliness-rivals-obesity-smoking-as-health-risk.

Of course, when team members are pitted in competition against one another, it is impossible to create a warm and friendly environment where budding friendships can thrive. Leaders must, therefore, be cognizant of how perceived accolades, like financial rewards and praise, are distributed. If team members perceive a "zero sum game" where there are only so many bonuses to give or compliments to bestow, then teamwork will suffer, and independent work will prevail.

Instead, leaders should harness the benefits of competition by challenging the team to work together on projects and to outdo rival organizations. In these instances, the team's camaraderie, pride, and interdependence increase while internal rivalries are diminished.

The Dopamine-Social Media Mix-up

Unfortunately, our high-technology world has us behaving in ways that increase our social isolation, rather than increasing our connection to real human beings. Dopamine—the neurotransmitter that gets us to crave the coffee we smell—is also in charge of all of our excited feelings related to technology (for example, the rush of excitement one might feel after seeing that an important email is answered or the thrill that is experienced after posting a new picture to social media).

We get that elated feeling because our brain anticipates the rush of caffeine, the acceptance of an important work deal, or the affirmation in the form of "likes" from friends, family, and acquaintances regarding the beauty or humor of our posted picture.

Sadly, people have increased their dependence on getting momentary gratification from superficial human connections—like "likes"—in place of working on in-person relationships. Leaders may be as guilty as anyone else, but they need to redirect the team to focus on developing human relationships.

Encourage Connection

What can a leader do to create meaningful relationships among team members? The first order of business is to initiate a <u>no-technology rule</u> at specific times during team events. The mere presence of a laptop computer or a Smartphone can "lessen the quality of in-person conversation, lowering the amount of empathy that is exchanged."[68] Computers and phones represent the countless possible other things we could and should be doing—the other people we could be talking to or the plethora of news we might be missing. Technology distracts us from being present with the people in front of us and attentively listening to their news.

The second step leaders can take to increase social connectedness among team members is to encourage more collaborative work and rely on the <u>strengths</u> of each team member to designate duties related to this work. As previously noted in chapter 3 on feedback, people blossom when given work that is particularly suited to their skills, abilities, and talents. Employees who feel capable at doing their job are more likely to be engaged at work, confident about the skills they bring, and complimentary of their colleagues.

Finally, leaders who want to increase the authentic human connections that occur among team members need to schedule <u>quarterly</u> activities that support and sustain these relationships. Of course, the team "happy hour" is a longstanding tradition in some workplaces. It should be noted, however, that "happy hours" can unintentionally exclude workers who have pressing demands (like children, a spouse, or a crated animal) that await them at home. For

---

[68] Dickerson, Kelly. "Are Smartphones Killing Our Conversation Quality?" *LiveScience*, Purch, 18 July 2014, www.livescience.com/46817-smartphones-lower-conversation-quality.html.

this reason, leaders should make every effort to schedule workgroup events during the work day.

If the chosen time coincides with a meal, make sure that appealing food is provided for the team. Eating together builds camaraderie. Volunteering for a special cause, engaging in off-site team building activities (like an outside ropes course or an inside Escape Room experience), or learning something new as a team are all examples of events that build authentic human connections.

As we consider human connections at work, the premise that emotions impede a productive workplace is challenged. Some managers may balk at the need to be an emotionally understanding, strengths-focused, activities director for their team members. In all fairness, when managerial responsibilities are formally described, the offer does not list many of the duties noted above. However, these tips are what separate a manager from a leader. Leaders choose to participate in such activities to create human connections among team members and to create an environment where each team member feels valued and connected.

Summary

This chapter concludes the overview of FRESH leadership. Feedback, Rewards, Engagement, Service, and Human Connections are skills that can transform managers into leaders and groups of people working together into collaborative teams. The next two chapters will touch on additional skills that are essential for lifelong leaders to practice and master—an ability to compensate for blind spots and a commitment to grow.

Turning New Knowledge into Results

The questions below are posed to help leaders and their team members gauge the level of human connection within the team and their ability to express their emotions at work.

Leader Self-Examination Questions

1. Do you apologize, model desirable work-balance behaviors, discuss failures, and ask for help from your team? Over the next four weeks, make a conscious effort to engage in these activities in front of the team.

2. Do you tend to be a Vulcan at work or an emotionally astute leader? Do you associate emotions at work with weakness? If so, why? Do you suspect that some of your team members might think you are "soft" if you start discussing emotions in a team setting? How could you combat this misconception?

3. Consider the questions in the loneliness quiz found in appendix F. Do you ever feel lonely? Do you worry that some of your team members are lonely? How might you help one team member who is more frequently excluded from group gatherings?

Group Discussion Questions

1. On a scale of 1 to 5 (with 1 being terrible and 5 being terrific), rate your ability to express your emotions at work.

2. What do you think happens when emotions are suppressed? Although some people wishfully believe suppressed emotions go away, research shows that suppressed emotions can fester

and negatively impact work performance and working relationships. When has understanding the emotions of a colleague helped you become a better co-worker?

3. Spending time together as a team and learning more about each other as people is important. What nonwork-related team activities have you most enjoyed in the past? What new activities would you like to try?

SECTION THREE

Chapter Eight

WHO'S GOT YOUR BLIND SPOTS?

*Every organization should tolerate rebels who
tell the emperor he has no clothes.*
–Colin Powell, former United States Secretary of State

In the quote above, Colin Powell refers to the classic Hans Christian Anderson fable, "The Emperor's New Clothes." The fable is about a vain and clothes-loving emperor who requests that a new, better, and more imperial outfit be created for him. The pompous emperor has some obvious insecurities and, like many insecure people in power, he has surrounded himself with staff who puff up his delicate ego, defer to his questionable wisdom, and tell him what he wants to hear.

The insecurities of the emperor have made him vulnerable to a pair of deceptive and conniving weavers who spin a dramatic tale and convince the emperor that they have the most remarkable fabric for his new attire. This newly created cloth is so refined and fantastic that it can only be seen by staff who are "fit for their post" but is invisible to those who are unfit for their positions.

Although the weavers never make any new clothes, they convince the emperor and his staff that they have constructed a remarkable new ensemble and pretend to dress the emperor in his new invisible getup. No one—not the emperor or his staff—admits that they see nothing, due to each person's individual embarrassment and belief that the rest of the group must, in fact, see what he or she does not. At last, a child who doesn't know any better, declares, "But he (the emperor) isn't wearing anything at all!"

The moral of this fable is clear—as is Colin Powell's reference to it—collective denial is dangerous. Real leaders want to know the difficult truths about themselves and the organization. For that reason, leaders surround themselves with team members who are wise enough to see what the leader cannot.

Managers are more likely to surround themselves with team members who do not challenge their perspectives, and those who do not confront uncomfortable or unsaid truths. In the "Emperor's New Clothes," the pretentiousness of the emperor is as troubling as is his comfort creating a safe, agreeable bubble around himself. Colin Powell advises that leaders need more than a team of safe "yes" people; they need candid "have you thought about this?" people.

Being a Leader in Life

In the previous five chapters, the FRESH perspective on leadership has been explained. These chapters, and the examples within them, have focused primarily on the skills needed from leaders in the corporate world today. My understanding of organizational behavior research coupled with my real-world interactions with business leaders has led me to believe that these five skills are essential practices needed from leaders who work for high-performing and dynamic organizations.

The next two chapters touch on the importance of compensating for our blind spots and pushing ourselves out of our comfort zones to learn and grow at every stage in life. These skills are necessary for leadership at work and at home. They help us to be better people at the height of our careers, but also as we embrace retirement. These skills can help leaders connect with their increasingly diverse flock but can also help senior leaders from becoming one-dimensional, stuck-in-their-ways, and, frankly, irrelevant.

All Drivers Have Blind Spots

Did you want to ride shot gun? Sorry, not an option. If you're leading, you're driving, and that means leaders are always driving. It's a leader's responsibility to move the team in the right direction. While doing this, they need to be constantly assessing their environment to identify and compensate for the unexpected—what I call their blind spots.

Drivers encounter a blind spot when a neighboring car hovers in the next lane but lags just a bit—just out of the driver's peripheral vision. It's annoying, but as experienced drivers, we understand the need to adjust and accommodate to the driving habits of others while at the same time reminding ourselves not to change lanes. The same is true of leaders. When we have blind spots, we must remember to accommodate those around us.

Blind spots in leadership can take many forms, but what they have in common is that, though occurring frequently, they are nonetheless unanticipated. Typically, this occurs because they introduce a completely different perspective or understanding of a situation. For instance, awareness of a blind spot could surface because individuals on the team feels excluded when they are not asked to a specific meeting, or another person is intimidated by the multiple fact-finding questions a leader asks.

As was discussed in *Unstuck at Last: Using Your Strengths to Get What You Want*, blind spots are something everyone—leader or not—can manage around. The best way to do so is to seek the perspective of someone else; ideally, a person who can clearly see what we cannot. This person will understand the root of our blind spots as well as the cause for disconnecting with, or even offending, a team member.

As a coach, I've noticed a high correlation between leaders' strengths and their blind spots (similar to the idea that someone's greatest strength can also be their greatest weakness). For example, one leader's strategic desire to have small meetings—without tangential departments involved—might offend an individual who prefers to be included in as many meetings as possible. In this situation, the leader is blind to the idea that small meetings can signal exclusivity to some.

Another leader's deft ability to probe for more answers and press for more details may be interpreted by a team member as a lack of confidence in the team. This leader is blind to how her need for more information may be interpreted as questioning the analysis put forth by the team.

Leaders, unlike managers, accept the idea that some issues might blindside them because they have a particular perspective. Leaders need to be on the lookout for partners who can candidly share a 360-degree perspective and help them avoid unnecessary collisions with their team members.

A good example of how a complementary partnership can work is found in chapter 5 between Dave and Nancy, his administrative assistant. Nancy helped Dave improve as a leader by identifying the team members' perception of him as overly intense. She suggested an option that would help Dave better connect with his team and then proactively scheduled one-on-one meetings with each team member.

In a small, more personal setting, Nancy was sure that Dave would connect with each individual, and his true personality would shine. Such a valuable partnership can only blossom when a leader is humble enough to accept such constructive feedback and when a peer or (in Nancy's case) a subordinate is brave enough to give it.

Experienced leaders frequently know where their weaknesses lie. Of course, additional insight and understanding about less-than-stellar traits can be found quite readily by taking the Clifton Strengths report and then looking at the last ten strengths on the "All 34" section. Typically, this portion of the report allows leaders to put words to the gaps in their abilities and, more importantly, discusses finding partners to help them manage around their inadequacies.

A great example of how to make one's awareness of a weakness into an opportunity for a new partnership with a peer or subordinate comes from Mark, a successful and insightful leader.

Mark, a leader of leaders, gathered his executive team to discuss their strengths and, ultimately, move their division to new heights. Mark considers himself a straight shooter who has had success in similar leadership roles because he was able to teach his high-performing managers to be forward-thinkers, patterns finders, and individuals who could deliver when the stakes were high.

Mark is confident in his abilities but aware of his weaknesses. He is aware that some might consider him intimidating and emotionally disconnected. He recognizes that he might be criticized by others for implementing cutting-edge techniques instead of being satisfied with incremental improvements. He is cognizant of the fact that he can have a difficult time celebrating success because he has moved on to the next new challenge.

What makes Mark a true leader, as opposed to a well-paid manager with a great title and a lot of power, is his willingness to ask his direct reports to help him in areas that are not his strengths. Mark used a portion of our time at the off-site "strengths" meeting to highlight his weaknesses, commend his team members who have helped him overcome his blind spots in the past, and solicit future help from each member of his entire team. Mark's openness about needing help to improve his weaknesses and his appreciation for team members who help him creates an environment where team members can feel comfortable and accepted when seeking help.

Who Challenges You Most?

In grade school, middle school, and high school, there was always one classmate who asked the most questions and had the most unusual and unlikely issues with the teacher. Your teacher probably dubbed this student "the problem child," though they would never have openly admitted that these students were driving them crazy.

Every non-problematic student in the class knew who "the problem children" were and how they annoyed their teachers on a daily basis. Many of us also learned at an early age not to ask the same questions posed by these challenging and often exasperating classmates.

When we graduated to a professional working environment, we quickly realized that the same "problem children" exist in grown-up form on our teams, and they challenged our managers in ways similar to how they challenged our past teachers. These troublesome employees ask questions, frequently express dissatisfaction with the way things at work are done and dispute the thinking of their managers. They seem to find conflict where others see none.

Swap Negative Intent for Positive Reframing

Today's young teachers are taught that such conflict in their classrooms should be addressed using positive intent. In fact, Dr. Becky Bailey advises in her book, *Conscious Discipline: Building Resilient Classrooms*, that teachers see these conflicts as an opportunity to help their students solve a problem—instead of finding fault, blaming, or labeling these students as "problem children."[69]

Today's leaders should do the same. Although assuming positive intent can be difficult and even maddening when dealing with employees who seem to constantly have a gripe, the benefits of doing so are enormous. Finding fault and labeling these challenging employees as problems, instead of looking for the opportunity to make positive organizational changes, is the sign of a mediocre manager, not a real leader. Squeaky-wheel employees may see issues that are invisible to the leader.

Reframing intent from negative to positive is a skill both teachers and leaders need to learn and practice on a regular basis. Our thoughts are frequently transparent. Thoughts can be interpreted by noting facial expression, tone of voice, and the kinds of words used.

Below are examples of how teachers and leaders can shift thoughts with negative intent by using positive reframing.

---

[69] Bailey, Rebecca Anne. *Conscious Discipline: Building Resilient Classrooms*. Loving Guidance, 2014.

Teacher's Negative Intent	Teacher's Positive Reframing
1. Susan sure knows how to drive me crazy.	1. Susan is emotionally perceptive and needs validation.
2. Al's disrupting the whole class.	2. Al has a lot of energy and needs help to stay on track.

Manager's Negative Intent	Leader's Positive Reframing
3. Sally always interrupts me when I'm really getting something done.	3. I should close my door if I cannot be interrupted. Sally appreciates my feedback. I need to schedule regular 1:1 meetings with her if I want to prevent interruptions.
4. Mark refuses to initiate discussions during our team meetings. He's not a team player.	4. Mark has great insights but seems hesitant to offer his opinion when the group meets. I need to talk to Mark about this. It may help if I give him an agenda early. He seems to do best when he has prep time.

In these examples, negative intent creates a wedge between the student and teacher or the leader and teammate. By positively reframing the situation, the teacher and leader can productively impact and potentially redirect the situation. When leaders assume negative intent, they place blame on others and are stuck. They cannot move forward. When leaders use positive intent, they identify the issue, accept joint responsibility in fixing the problem, and can redirect future behavior.

Empower the Team's Introvert

In the fourth example on the preceding page, the reframing example is related to how a manager might negatively interpret the actions of a quiet team member. The positive reframing shows how a leader can flip a negative label such as "not a team player" into an opportunity to help this quiet team member effectively participate in the team's group discussions.

Great leaders know how to engage introverted team members and spark their less attention-needy personalities. In Susan Cain's book *Quiet: The Power of Introverts in a World That Can't Stop Talking*, she explains how the insights and knowledge of introverts can be greatly diminished in a world that values extroverts.[70] Leaders can address the problematic issue of overlooking introverts by creating strong personal connections with the introverts on the team. The introvert of a group may be able to articulate in a private conversation issues that are invisible to many but important to the function of the team.

Leaders who have a good understanding of and appreciation for the expertise of their team's introvert may be able to draw the introvert into the group's discussion more readily. By posing particular questions (for example, "Bill, I know you have done some special training in this area. What are your thoughts?"), a leader can simultaneously empower the team's introvert and signal to the rest of the team that even the quieter team members have worthwhile insights.

64% of workers believe their organization doesn't fully utilize the unique talents of introverts.[71]

---

[70] Cain, Susan. *Quiet: the Power of Introverts in a World That Can't Stop Talking.* Penguin Books, 2013

[71] Bruce, Jan. "Unleash Your Team's Full Potential: A Guide To Introverts In The Office." *Forbes*, Forbes Magazine, 17 Feb. 2017, www.forbes.com/sites/janbruce/2017/02/17/unleash-your-teams-full-potential-a-guide-to-introverts-in-the-office/.

Beware: The Curse of Knowledge

Dan and Chip Heath, brothers and co-authors of *Made to Stick: Why Some Ideas Last and Others Don't*, are great story-tellers and are also responsible for shining a bright light on the dimly understood phenomena of the curse of knowledge—another potential blind spot for leaders.[72] In short, this curse is responsible for a host of communications issues that can occur at work, including: overwhelming new hires, confusing customers who don't understand industry-specific language, and frustrating managers who cannot connect organizational mission statements to what behaviors should be demonstrated.

The curse of knowledge occurs when we make the assumption that our audience has the same perspective and knowledge that we do. Imagine you're not a software engineer but end up in a research and development meeting where they are discussing in great detail how to revamp the latest version of the company's mobile app technology. It could sound like they were speaking a different language.

While this may seem an extreme example, it illustrates the curse of knowledge. It can create unnecessary misunderstandings when the listener misinterprets or doesn't understand the terms being used. This gap between what's being said and what's heard can happen in any area where industry-specific or specialized information is communicated.

Leaders, many of whom are specialists, are frequently required to summarize information for others which makes them disproportionately susceptible to the curse of knowledge. When presenting a supremely familiar topic, it can be difficult to remember what it's like to have little or zero knowledge about it. Since everyone

---

[72] Heath, Chip, and Dan Heath. *Made to Stick: Why Some Ideas Survive and Others Die.* Random House, 2010.

in our daily orbit knows and speaks the same language, it may be hard to remember that others do not know this language. When the people who surround a leader do not want to appear stupid, the curse of knowledge can go unchecked and dominate the way we communicate, despite its lack of effectiveness.

Successfully overcoming the curse of knowledge requires leaders to translate large sweeping statements into actionable, concrete, and practical items for their team. For example, The Ritz-Carlton is known for wanting to delight its customers. In fact, The Ritz-Carlton CEO Horst Schulze has said, "Unless you have 100 percent satisfaction … you must improve."

Similarly, Jeff Bezos, founder and CEO of Amazon, has said, "We see our customers as invited guests to a party, and we are the hosts. It's our job every day to make every important aspect of the customer experience a little bit better."[73] In both instances, these CEOs could use platitudes like "Delight our customers," or "Customer service is our number one priority," but they choose to use a concrete goal (100% satisfaction) and a clear metaphor (we are hosts!) to illustrate their points.

New hires—especially those from different industries or with little industry-specific knowledge—can be a great resource for uncovering how well an organization has avoided the curse of knowledge. When communication during the first few weeks on the job is unclear, newly hired employees can feel overwhelmed and uncertain. Leaders should proactively ask new hires for their fresh perspective on how language is used during the on-boarding process, in their first meetings, or even

---

[73] Greathouse, John. "5 Time-Tested Success Tips From Amazon Founder Jeff Bezos." *Forbes*, Forbes Magazine, 4 May 2013, www.forbes.com/sites/johngreathouse/2013/04/30/5-time-tested-success-tips-from-amazon-founder-jeff-bezos/.

on the organization's website. The leader opens the door to a candid conversation about the need to eliminate confusing work-speak.

New customers can also give insight into this tricky communication issue. No one wants to insult a customer by presuming they have less knowledge than they do. However, the opposite is also true. No one wants to confuse a customer and presume they are well acquainted with industry-specific knowledge when they are not.

Transparent conversations are necessary between an organizational representative and customer to prevent any possible misunderstandings related to organizational jargon. One way to ensure communications remain clear is to give new customers concrete explanations and/or visual aids to add clarity. Another way is to use past customer issues as a starting place for a new conversation. For example, a representative could explain, "Last week, I was working on a project, and we realized that our organizations referred to the following issues differently…."

Leaders need to proactively address the curse of knowledge by fighting the urge to use industry-specific jargon and, instead, use concrete examples as much as possible when talking to other leaders, team members, customers, and the public.

Summary

This chapter, on blind spots, reminds us that good leaders are not all-knowing but are expert at knowing what they don't know, finding the right people to help them see the world from a different perspective, and accepting the advice and insights they receive. Assuming negative intent when working with others or adopting the notion that all introverts are less-than-ideal team players are mistakes made by unskilled managers, not seasoned leaders. Identifying blind spots can be difficult.

Turning New Knowledge into Results

The questions below are posed with the hope that leaders and their teams can talk openly about them, and like new drivers, gain experience managing around their blind spots.

Leader Self-Examination Questions

1. What are your potential blind spots? Frequently, our blind spots are connected to our strengths and our weaknesses. For example:
   - Do you have difficulty asking for help?
   - Do you assume your vast knowledge base will always trump the insights of a less-experienced team member?
   - Do you avoid conflict?
   - Do you look for conflict?
   - Do you blame others instead of taking blame?
   - Do you deemphasize feelings and focus only on facts?
   - Are you a perfectionist?
   - Do you settle for good when great is possible?

2. Who has challenged you most in the past? How did you respond? In a perfect world, how would you have responded? How can you learn to be more accepting of the "problem child/children" on your team?

3. Do you have an introvert on your team? Have you discussed ways for them to feel more comfortable voicing their opinions during group meetings? How can you become more proactive

in helping this team member engage with the team more frequently?

4. How might awareness of your blind spots help you grow as a person? Do you have a best friend, spouse, or relative that helps you see yourself and the world with more clarity?

Group Discussion Questions

1. Do you have any blind spots? Many times, spouses or good friends are able to see very clearly the things that are invisible to us. Do you have an example of this? Is there anyone at work who you rely upon to help you see yourself or your blind spots better?

2. What kinds of blind spots might we have as a team? When we use language that is specific to our industry or our product, can we be misunderstood or confusing to our customers? Let's create a list of the most problematic phrases and terms for people. Let's also create a list of alternatives to these phrases and terms.

Chapter Nine
GROW OR DIE

Anyone who stops learning is old, whether at twenty or eighty. Anyone who keeps learning stays young.
–Henry Ford, founder of the Ford Motor company

I vividly remember the pain shooting through my legs during the summer before I started my freshman year in high school. I was growing. My parents assured me that this pain was both temporary and necessary to become the person I was destined to be. But it really hurt. Ultimately, I outgrew all of my pants, shorts, and dresses that summer. I was in the midst of an official growth spurt.

Growth, whether it be physical or cognitive, is a bit uncomfortable. The growing pains experienced as a child during a high-growth period are uncannily similar to the growing pains that can be experienced as an adult when learning something new. Both are uncomfortable, temporary, and necessary for development. I thoroughly agree with Henry Ford, in that, learning keeps one young. But I also try to remind myself and my coaching clients that being a youthful-in-spirit learner is sometimes painful.

Limiting Beliefs Can Limit Learning

After working with hundreds of coaching clients on long-term and short-term goals, I have found that limiting beliefs are the most frequent obstruction to growth, specifically related to learning. When a particular type of growth is desired, that growth is impossible if a client dismisses the possibility of reaching the goal. They might say that, "I'm too old to do that," or "I'll just hire a young person to do it for me," or "I'd feel/look/be foolish at my age doing something new like that."

Limiting beliefs only result in limited opportunities. By confronting these beliefs, the first step towards growth and new possibilities becomes attainable for leaders and their team members—regardless of age. The most memorable example I have of extinguishing a limiting belief occurred when I was working with a leader in the financial sales industry.

When I met Todd, he was at the top of his game professionally. Todd had great aptitude when it came to connecting with people, winning them over, and influencing their behaviors. Undoubtedly, Todd had perfected these skills as a kid. He quickly learned how to capitalize on his gregarious personality and athleticism to make friends at the multiple schools he attended during his youth—five schools located in four different cities over the span of five years. While multiple school changes might have challenged another child, Todd thrived in this dynamic social environment.

However, Todd was frustrated and disheartened after a few years of attending college classes. He was not engaged in the classroom. He did not enjoy the grind of reading, studying, and taking exams—although he greatly enjoyed the community and congeniality of the campus.

Ultimately, Todd left college to start working in a profession where he knew he would have success: sales.

Todd made the reasonable and healthy choice to free himself from his miserable commitment to become a college graduate. The only long-term negative ramification that resulted from this choice was Todd's limiting belief that resulted from this choice. He came to believe that he was not a good reader or learner. This belief was limiting Todd's ability to become a better person, a better leader, and a better employee.

After many years of subscribing to this limiting belief, I asked Todd about his goals—what did he want to strive for, and how could he stretch himself in new ways? His response was filled with a rare candor and sincerity. Todd wanted to become a reader. He had an enormous respect for people who reeled off interesting information that they had garnered from a hot new business book or an older classic.

He was embarrassed that he could not force himself to sit down and read a book from start to finish. Todd did not yearn for an undergraduate degree or any form of "proof" that he was smart and successful. He just wanted access to the same topical and relevant information that his friends and colleagues inserted into daily conversations; information they frequently found in books.

Todd's limiting belief was, "Reading is the only **real** way to obtain current and meaningful information. I hate to read. Therefore, I must suffer the natural consequences of not liking to read." When I assured Todd that listening to a book on tape was as **real** as reading a book, he was dumbfounded. "Does listening to books count?" he asked. "Yes, of course it does," I responded.

In an instant, Todd had tossed away his limiting belief and gained access to a world of information that was forbidden to him just moments before. Todd, now in his early fifties, is an honest-to-goodness reader (ok, literally, he's a listener). Since that turning-point revelation, since that day when Todd let go of his limiting belief, our coaching sessions have become filled with enthusiastic discussions of new books we might want to read and the rehashing of older books we have both enjoyed.

The impact of this shift in perspective has been profound. Todd is no longer a "wishful reader." He incorporates his newfound book learning into presentations, everyday conversations, and sales calls. He is more assured in his current career and that he will achieve his long-term, post-career goals. Before, Todd's limiting belief made him question his current success and his opportunity for continued success. Now, due to Todd's ability to overcome his limiting belief, he has been transformed into a confident and proud learner.

Examples of limiting beliefs are vast. In this example, Todd's limiting belief was connected to how he understood himself and his own abilities. It is important to note that limiting beliefs are not always related to ourselves and our self-identity, nor are they always easy to overcome.

My guess is that every reader has encountered a person with limiting beliefs related to money, relationships, love, weight loss, or time—to name just a few limiting beliefs that can sabotage us. It can be difficult to change these familiar thoughts ("I'll always be broke."), because they become routine and safe, despite being contrary to our best interests.

Generally, our human tendency is to choose familiar misery over an unknown happiness. This makes many limiting beliefs difficult to overcome. Todd's open-mindedness allowed him to revise his long-standing belief that he was not a reader. His ability to recognize that listening to a book on tape was as valid as reading a book was instrumental to his seemingly effortless success.

Model the Right Learning Behaviors

Leaders, unlike managers, challenge themselves and others to eschew limiting beliefs and embrace the discomforts of growth. Leaders know that limiting beliefs are merely mechanisms that hinder success. They know that the benefits of acquiring new knowledge are greater than the pain of growth. Leaders inspire personal and professional growth in their team members by modeling the right behaviors.

However, there are times when growth, from a team member's perspective, can feel like jumping out of a plane without a parachute—terrifying. No one at work wants to admit to ignorance or deficiency. Occasionally, I encounter team members who are resistant to learning new things because "the way we do things now works just fine." Agreeing to the idea that there is room for improvement can be humbling. Learning something new—a new technique, a new process, a new computer program—may infer that the current processes are lacking. Of course, this can be an uncomfortable admission to make at work.

A leader's job is to assure each team member that the parachute is there, strapped to his or her back; the ripcord is hanging at-the-ready to deploy the canopy; and a safe landing is guaranteed.

Below are a few examples of how leaders can create an environment that encourages growth and learning while also providing safety for team members who are encountering new, and possibly uncomfortable, growth.

Learn from failure

Many leaders believe failure is a natural phenomenon that occurs prior to success. Celebrating failure because it signifies that success is close at hand is a leap … but it is a leap some leaders are willing to make. Those of us who are more skeptical about the benefits of throwing a big failure celebration can try a different tactic. Instead of celebrating failure, analyze it. Spend time deconstructing and demystifying the origins of a failure so that it makes more sense.

Unearthing the who, what, why, and how of a failure empowers the leader and the team. Asking these questions is a key aspect of recovering from the shock and remorse that failure inevitably brings. Coming away from failure with insight and power is a gift. Notably, such a gift is only possible when a talented leader can shift the ennui of failure to the perspective of learning.

Learn about and engage in new technology
Leaders need to not only do as they say but also act as they say. When relating this statement to technology, it means, "Use the same technology you are championing and forcing your team to use." There's a difference between believing in the benefits of technology and forcing oneself to learn how to use it. It's important to understand firsthand the benefits that are possible because of new technology.

Be curious about the world—both past and future
Globalization is the idea that all nations and societies are more interdependent than ever before. This concept should spur leaders to be curious about the world—where it has been, and where it is going. Globalization and new technology impact the way we work, what we eat, how we travel, who we talk to, and how we spend every minute of every day.

Leaders need to recognize that this global interdependence will only become more prevalent in the coming years. Learning how the world arrived where it is today and better understanding where it is headed in the future allows a leader to be in the driver's seat, anticipating change as opposed to reacting to it.

Be curious about people
What's the special magic that each team member brings to group work? If asked, most individuals can categorize themselves into one of the following four groups: do-ers (work focused), planners (strategy focused), people pleasers (emotion focused), or guiders (influence focused).

On multiple occasions, when it looks like our travel plans have been disrupted due to weather or mechanical errors, my husband has said to me "go work your magic." It's his abbreviated way of saying, "Go convince that ticketing agent over there to let us on the next flight, since our current flight just got cancelled, and there are no other flights out tonight. If you can get us upgraded, that'd be nice too." I'm a guider who loves to be given the opportunity to influence the behaviors of others.

When team members can harness their own special magic for the good of the team, great things happen. Combining your curiosity and interest with your team's magical powers is a recipe for success.

Be curious about yourself
Socrates said, "To know thyself is the beginning of wisdom." Leaders need to model an open-minded desire to continually learn about themselves. Knowledge is power, and self-knowledge is a powerful component of leadership. Understanding your strengths, your values, your interests, your temperament, and your mission in life will help you to stay on course to achieve the goals that are most fulfilling.

Inspiring leaders recognize that these components of self-knowledge can act like a compass that keeps them centered and on track. It can also encourage the same curiosity about self in their team members.

Be curious about what's new
The differences between being fresh and being stale are vast. No one wants to eat a stale sandwich, listen to a stale joke, or drink a stale beer. Being fresh is synonymous with being new, different, modern, or forward-thinking. Being fresh is the antithesis of being conventional.

The conventional way to do something implies the use of a tried-and-true method. A fresh way to approach a task, such as leadership, implies that an all-new and possibly revolutionary process will be used.

Summary

Continuous growth and improvement are key aspects of being fresh, all-new, and even revolutionary. Leaders are aware of their competition and are keenly aware that their competition is learning and growing every day. As Henry Ford so aptly says in the quote that precedes this chapter, if we stop learning we become old … no matter our chronological age.

Turning New Knowledge into Results

Some individuals do not consider themselves to be learning-focused because they were not stellar students in high school or college. Through coaching, I have helped non-traditional learners (those who don't learn well by reading books or listening to lectures) to realize their non-traditional learning activities (like watching YouTube videos or using their Google app incessantly) are also valid means of learning. Remember to consider the traditional and non-traditional methods of learning you rely upon when answering the questions below.

Leader Self-Examination Questions

1. Do you consider yourself committed to learning? What topics are you most excited to learn more about? How do you find out more about these topics?
2. Do you have any limiting beliefs related to yourself or the world that may impact your ability to learn, grow, and lead?
3. Can you think of a failure that has positively impacted you? Have you ever shared this story with your team?

Group Discussion Questions

1. We have more access to information today than ever before. Sometimes it can be overwhelming. However, learning new things together can turn a boring or overwhelming situation into a fun and engaging opportunity. Create a list of your favorite YouTube or TedTalk videos, podcasts, books and articles that have taught you something in the last few years. How might we share our lists to learn more about each other and our world?
2. Do you have your own "special magic" that allows you to prevail in situations that are daunting to others?

Chapter Ten
FINAL THOUGHTS

The best way to predict your future is to create it.
—Abraham Lincoln

Leadership is not a solo activity that can be cultivated in the privacy of your office with the door closed or while driving alone to work. It is a hands-on, get-up-to-your-eyeballs-in-it affair. Leadership is defined as "a process by which a person influences **others** to accomplish an objective and directs the organization in a way that makes it more coherent and cohesive."[74]

It is not an easy road or a fixed destination. There will be difficulties along the way, challenges that require more grit than you think you have. Just when it seems you've got a handle on things, the playing field will likely change.

In spite of these difficulties, hang in there. The skills outlined in this book are a guide to put you and your team members on a new path. This path requires leaders to be a resource, a champion, and a spark that ignites the passions of others in a working environment operating under new rules.

---

[74] Hamilton, Marilyn. "How Building A Leadership Organization Prepares the Way for Learning." *Transforming Leadership*, 2017, 279-89. doi:10.1201/9780203735237-11.

Asking your team members to join you on this **F.R.E.S.H. path** is an important step towards becoming a **F.R.E.S.H. leader**. You cannot lead alone. Learning your team's thoughts and insights about the topics discussed in this book is the best way to transform you and your team and to catapult each and every one of you to new heights.

As you cultivate your new leadership skills and hone your old ones, keep the following ideas in mind:

Feedback is something 65% of employees wants more of—and both positive and negative feedback increases engagement.

Rewards are more than material things. They are also connected to values and can drive powerful internal motivators.

Engagement only happens for 33% of employees. Make sure your team members fall into this select group.

Service to the team, developing talents, and cultivating the strengths of team members are *privileges* of leadership.

Human connections occur when leaders are able to be vulnerable and authentic. Strong human connections make strong teams.

Best of luck to you and your team on this journey. Knowledge is power but knowledge without action is useless. Turn your new knowledge into results through open discussion and follow-through. Create a FRESH and bright future for you and your team.

Appendix A
BET AND BEAR

BET Method

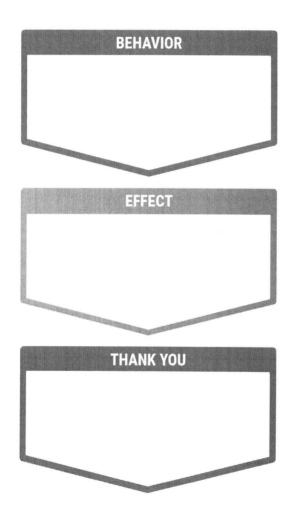

BEAR Method

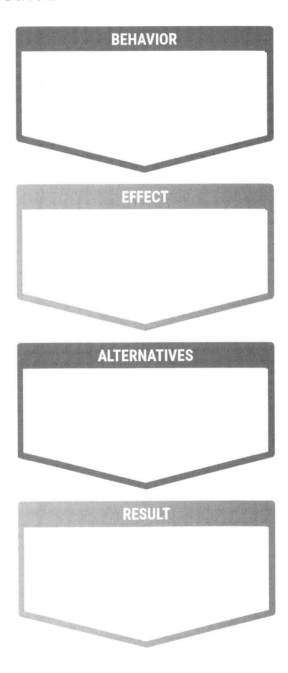

Appendix B
MOTIVATORS AT WORK

Using the list below, select your top five rewards from the entire list (both extrinsic and intrinsic) and rank these choices in order of importance (with #1 being the most important and #5 least).

Have your team members complete the same task. Discuss the importance of both extrinsic and intrinsic rewards at work.

Extrinsic Rewards – Reward Outside Self

- Salary
- Health benefits
- Paid vacation days
- Fringe benefits
- Promotion
- Security
- Nice work environment
- Training opportunities
- Awards
- Praise

Intrinsic Rewards – Reward Within Self

- Feeling satisfied
- Feeling capable
- Feeling appreciated
- Enjoyment from doing the task (which tasks are most enjoyable?)
- Satisfaction derived from accomplishments
- Satisfaction derived from realizing potential
- Satisfaction derived from leading others
- Work feels meaningful

Appendix C
AUTONOMY-MASTERY-PURPOSE

Leaders and team members can improve intrinsic motivation by focusing on these three components: autonomy, mastery, and purpose. Which of these three components is most important to you? Give yourself one point for each "yes" response and tally up your score. In which areas did you score the most and the least points?

AUTONOMY

1. Do you get to choose what you work on each day?
2. Do you get to choose how much time you spend on various activities?
3. Do you get to choose who you work with?
4. Do you get to choose how you perform your work?

MASTERY

1. Do you believe that you are getting better at the work you perform?
2. Are you hopeful that in ten years you will be closer to mastery of your job or the job you aspire to perform?
3. Do you believe that you will always be able to improve and grow in ability in your job?

PURPOSE

1. Do you believe your work is connected to a bigger purpose?
2. Do you feel pride in the work you do?

Adapted from "Pink's Autonomy, Mastery and Purpose Framework Encouraging Self-Motivation." *Groupthink - Decision Making Skills Training from MindTools.com,* Mind Tools, www.MindTools.com/pages/article/autonomy-mastery-purpose.htm.

Appendix D

WORK AND MEANING INVENTORY

Work can mean a lot of different things to different people. The following items ask you to consider the role of work in your own life. With 1 being least true and 5 most true, please indicate honestly how correct each statement is for you and your work.

1. I have found a meaningful career. 1 2 3 4 5
2. I view my work as contributing to my personal growth. 1 2 3 4 5
3. My work really makes no difference to the world. 1 2 3 4 5
4. I understand how my work contributes to my life's meaning. 1 2 3 4 5
5. I have a good sense of what makes my job meaningful. 1 2 3 4 5
6. I know my work makes a positive difference in the world. 1 2 3 4 5
7. My work helps me better understand myself. 1 2 3 4 5
8. I have discovered work that has a satisfying purpose. 1 2 3 4 5
9. My work helps me make sense of the world around me. 1 2 3 4 5
10. The work I do serves a greater purpose. 1 2 3 4 5

Scoring instructions.

- Add the ratings for items 1, 4, 5, and 8 to get the "Positive Meaning" score. The Positive Meaning scale reflects the degree to which people find their work to hold personal meaning, significance, or purpose.

- Add the ratings for items 2, 7, and 9 to get the "Meaning-Making through Work" score. The Meaning-Making through Work score reflects the fact that work is often a source of broader meaning in life for people, helping them to make sense of their life experience.

- Getting the "Greater Good Motivations" score involves a two-step process. First, subtract the item 3 rating from 6 (e.g., if a client gave item 3 a rating of 2, then their converted rating would be 4 [6-2=4]); then add this number to the ratings for items 6 and 10. The Greater Good Motivations score reflects the degree to which people see that their effort at work makes a positive contribution.

2011 Michael F. Steger. The Work and Meaning Inventory (WAMI) can be used in research and educational capacities without restriction. Permission for commercial or revenue-generating applications of the WAMI must be obtained from Michael F. Steger prior to use.

Appendix E

VALUES

Determine your core values. From the list below, choose and write down every core value that resonates with you. Do not overthink your selections.

As you read through the list, simply write down the words that feel like a core value to you personally. If you think of a value you possess that is not on the list, be sure to write it down as well.

Abundance	Caring	Decisiveness
Acceptance	Challenge	Dedication
Accountability	Charity	Dependability
Achievement	Cheerfulness	Diversity
Advancement	Cleverness	Empathy
Adventure	Community	Encouragement
Advocacy	Commitment	Enthusiasm
Ambition	Compassion	Ethics
Appreciation	Cooperation	Excellence
Attractiveness	Collaboration	Expressiveness
Autonomy	Consistency	Fairness
Balance	Contribution	Family
Being the Best	Creativity	Friendships
Benevolence	Credibility	Flexibility
Boldness	Curiosity	Freedom
Brilliance	Daring	Fun
Calmness		Generosity

Appendix

Grace	Originality	Reliability
Growth	Passion	Resilience
Flexibility	Performance	Resourcefulness
Happiness	Personal	Responsibility
Health	Development	Responsiveness
Honesty	Proactive	Security
Humility	Professionalism	Self-Control
Humor	Quality	Selflessness
Inclusiveness	Recognition	Simplicity
Independence	Risk	Stability
Individuality	Taking	Success
Innovation	Safety	Teamwork
Inspiration	Security	Thankfulness
Intelligence	Service	Thoughtfulness
Intuition	Spirituality	Traditionalism
Joy	Stability	Trustworthiness
Kindness	Peace	Understanding
Knowledge	Perfection	Uniqueness
Leadership	Playfulness	Usefulness
Learning	Popularity	Versatility
Love	Power	Vision
Loyalty	Preparedness	Warmth
Making a Difference	Proactivity	Wealth
Mindfulness	Professionalism	Well-Being
Motivation	Punctuality	Wisdom
Optimism	Recognition	Zeal
Open-Mindedness	Relationships	

Values Exercise adapted from TAPROOT—
www.TapRoot.com/archives/3777.

Appendix F
LONELINESS QUIZ[75]

For each question, please indicate the answer that best represents your on-the-spot belief about each question. This takes most people about three minutes to complete. Take your time and answer truthfully for the most accurate results.

1. How often do you feel unhappy doing so many things alone?
   - Never
   - Rarely
   - Sometimes
   - Often

2. How often do you feel you have nobody to talk to?
   - Never
   - Rarely
   - Sometimes
   - Often

3. How often do you feel you cannot tolerate being so alone?
   - Never
   - Rarely
   - Sometimes
   - Often

---

[75] "The Loneliness Quiz." Psych Central. Accessed January 11, 2019. https://psychcentral.com/quizzes/loneliness-quiz/.

4. How often do you feel as if nobody really understands you?
   - Never
   - Rarely
   - Sometimes
   - Often

5. How often do you find yourself waiting for people to call or write?
   - Never
   - Rarely
   - Sometimes
   - Often

6. How often do you you feel completely alone?
   - Never
   - Rarely
   - Sometimes
   - Often

7. How often do you feel you are able to reach out and communicate with those around you?
   - Never
   - Rarely
   - Sometimes
   - Often

8. How often do you feel starved for company?
    - Never
    - Rarely
    - Sometimes
    - Often
9. How often do you feel it is difficult for you to make friends?
    - Never
    - Rarely
    - Sometimes
    - Often
10. How often do you feel shut out and excluded by others?
    - Never
    - Rarely
    - Sometimes
    - Often

Scoring

Give yourself a 1 for every Never, a 2 for every Rarely, a 3 for every Sometimes, and a 4 for every Often response.

Scoring Key:

If you scored	You may have
30 and up	Extreme loneliness
22-29	Moderate loneliness
15-12	Normal loneliness
10-14	Little to no loneliness

This is not a diagnostic tool. This loneliness quiz is based upon a multitude of research that centers around a shortened version of Russell, D. (1996). The UCLA Loneliness Scale (Version 3): Reliability, validity, and factor structure. *Journal of Personality Assessment*, 66, 20-40. All rights reserved. For personal, educational or research use only; other use may be prohibited by law.

Thank You

Thank you for your willingness to read FRESH Leadership. Your curiosity and desire to learn something new are commendable!

I am deeply grateful to my colleagues, students, friends, and family who have encouraged me to share my organizational behavior knowledge and my consulting experiences. Combining these talents has indelibly marked and thoroughly shaped my understanding of leadership. Thank you to the many individuals who shared their stories and helped transform what might have been a mundane passage (e.g., defining a limiting belief) into something that I hope was memorable and interesting (e.g., learning how Todd gained a love of reading at 50 years old).

Please share this book with others—leaders, students of leadership, would-be leaders, and teams that look forward to being propelled into the future by the fresh thoughts of their leader. The old work rules are dead. My profound wish is that this book helps to bridge the gap between the old and the new.

Feedback is welcome. No one ever got better in a vacuum, right? Write an online review, send a personal note, or just make a phone call. Your suggestions for improvement, your ah-ha moments of insight, and your thoughts about how to support new FRESH leaders are just a few examples of how you can facilitate my growth, curiosity, and desire to keep learning.

My sincere thanks!
Sarah

Sarah@FreshConceptsOnline.com
FreshConceptsOnline.com
UnstuckAtLast.com

Please connect with me on LinkedIn: LinkedIn.com/in/Sarah-Robinson-05499427

About the Author

Sarah Robinson is a Gallup-Certified Strengths Coach and the best-selling author of *Unstuck at Last: Using Your Strengths to Get What You Want*. For more than 20 years, she has performed organizational development training for a variety of companies in the for-profit and non-profit fields. In 2013, Sarah was among the first of seven consultants worldwide to be certified by Gallup as an Individual and Team Coach using the CliftonStrengthsFinder assessment. In 2015, she became one of the first to be trained by Gallup to use the BP10, a feedback tool designed to develop the strengths needed to be an entrepreneur.

Sarah's "Top 5 Signature Themes" are Competition, Maximizer, Achiever, Activator, and Significance. She translates these natural strengths into obtaining measurable results for her clients and helping them get "Unstuck at Last"—both professionally and personally.

In addition to her Gallup training and certification, Sarah holds a Master's in Industrial and Organizational Psychology; the designation of Professional in Human Resources (PHR) from the Society of Human Resources Management (SHRM); and the position of Associate Faculty Member at IUPUI.

Sarah is known for her enthusiasm—in the classroom, as a presenter, and as a Strengths Coach. She enjoys meeting her clients' needs while challenging herself to learn more about the ever-growing discipline of organizational behavior. Sarah lives with her family and ill-behaved, but extremely handsome, chocolate Labrador Retriever in Carmel, Indiana.

ALSO FROM BEST-SELLING AUTHOR

SARAH ROBINSON

Unstuck at Last guides individuals and corporate teams on a path to find their true calling, optimize their productivity, and even deal with change.

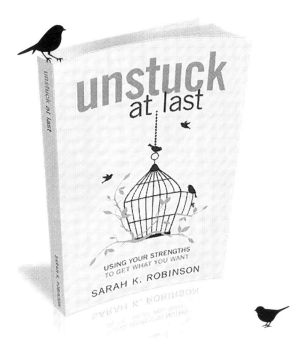

No one wants to be stuck.

Learn how to tap into your full potential and unlock your dreams.

Made in the USA
Middletown, DE
10 March 2019